ZEN
ATHLETE

MATTHEW BELAIR

*"Within a month of reading and applying Zen Athlete's practical
and user-friendly training techniques, I set two world records!"*
-Brodie Carmichael (Freestyle Motocross Rider)

The secrets to achieving your highest potential.

The Secrets to Achieving Your Highest Potential

Matthew Belair

DEDICATION

I would like to dedicate this book to my amazing, loving parents, Sarah and Michel Belair. Thank you for always believing in me no matter what! This is also dedicated to my family, friends, and to all of the people who have supported me over the years, all my love! Finally, this book is dedicated to you, the reader. I admire you for taking the action necessary to push your limits and discover how powerful you really are!

The first and
best victory is to
conquer self.

–Plato

TABLE OF CONTENTS

PREFACE

Armed with a red karate bandana, nun chucks, and a plethora of martial arts movies, my journey had already begun, and I didn't even know it. I can vividly remember my eight-year-old self watching martial art movies with almost obsessive repetition. My favorite martial artist by far was, and still is, Bruce Lee. I would watch in awe of his talent and physical abilities, as he would continuously blow my mind with extraordinary feats of strength, speed, and skill. It was my interest in him and martial arts that lead me to the question I have been attempting to find the answer to ever since: What am I capable of? Furthermore what are humans capable of?

Humans continually accomplish feats that defy logic and science. A few examples are Master Guo my Sifu from China who could break granite with two fingers; Olympic athletes who continually break records of speed and strength; or snowboarders, skiers, free-runners, gymnasts, and extreme sports athletes who continually push themselves to the limit. It is an irrefutable fact that the mind-body connection is paramount for anyone who wants to accomplish anything that is at an elite level, ground breaking, mind blowing, or revolutionary. It is the same mind-body connection that decides the limits you put on yourself in your daily life.

My research into the power of the mind to discover how exactly a person is able to accomplish things that are thought to be impossible has taken me down countless paths, and I have noticed various overlapping principles that are the basis of achieving full potential. This book is a combination of neuro-linguistic programming (NLP), sport psychology, visualization, martial arts, yoga techniques, and a few other powerful and effective tools and information. Only tried, tested, and proven strategies are contained within this manual and when applied will force you to reach your highest potential. All of the unnecessary filler has been filtered out to bring you a clear, concise, practical, and immensely effective performance model. Upon completion of this book you will be armed with the best and most effective mental training strategies that you can apply to sport and life!

I would like to thank you, the reader, for giving me a chance to share my passion. It is my sincerest desire that this information help you improve your athletic performance in a profound way and, more importantly, cause you to realize the infinite power you hold within and help you harness it for all your future pursuits.

I wish you all the success in the world, and may love, peace, and joy fill your life.

Matthew Belair

INTRODUCTION

Real Life Super Humans and
How to Get the Most Out of This Book

*If you really want to do something,
you'll find a way. If you don't you'll find an excuse.*
—Jim Rohn

During the last decade extreme sports progression has been pushed past limits that few of us had thought were possible. Athletes are doing what they're supposed to; they are evolving the sport one season at a time. The things you believe about yourself, the thoughts you think, and the decisions you make ultimately make up your life. Therefore it must be your decision to choose to excel at athletics and your sport. Within these pages, you'll find a complete guide of simple and powerful strategies that, if applied and worked at, will yield astounding results. Although what you'll be learning may seem simple I have found one underlying common denominator between all athletes who have outperformed their peers and set the bar for others to strive towards, and that is hard work.

Simply reading this book will not do you any service; it is only in the application of the tools you'll be learning that will generate results. Bruce Lee once said, "Knowing is not enough, we must apply; willing is not enough, we must do." He knew that without the application of knowledge, the knowledge itself would be useless. Sport psychology has exploded in popularity during the last 20 years and continues to grow because athletes are not only recognizing it gets results they are realizing and understanding that applying the material is essential if they are to reach their full potential.

I am not going to waste my words in this book trying to convince you mental training works because it does, and every elite-level athlete knows it. Jack Nicklaus, Michael Jordan, George St-Pierre and countless others use it, and you probably wouldn't be reading this if you didn't think it worked.

Far more important than sport psych is the realization of the power of the mind and the unlimited power you possess within. Once you have come to understand that the mind has unlimited potential you must reach the ultimate conclusion that you too hold that power, and you must believe in yourself because no one else can ever do that for you. There are literally thousands of incredible stories and studies that prove our minds are infinitely powerful, and they can do things that are scientifically supposed to be impossible.

A great example of a modern superhuman is Wim Hof who holds 21 Guinness World Records, including running a marathon in the Arctic circle wearing only sandals and shorts. Conversely, he ran a full marathon in the Namib desert without water consumption. Science tells us that our autonomic nervous system cannot be controlled by our own free will, however Wim is able to maintain a steady internal body temperature even after sitting for 1 hour and 52 minutes in freezing cold water and ice. Wim achieves this through a breathing pattern, meditation, and by willing his mind. This leaves scientists baffled ("The beginning of the Iceman" 2016).

The power of the mind is undeniable and you must believe in your own potential or no amount of evidence will convince you. You are capable of great things, and when you decide that you want to achieve greatness in sport and in life you can feel great knowing that hard work, dedication, and belief in yourself will always produce results. The processes are made simple so that you can apply them instantly and easily. It is up to you to choose excellence or mediocrity. Once you decide what it is you truly want from athletics or life, simply believe in yourself, and go get it!

This book is formatted and written in such a way that you will have an easy time retaining and applying all of the strategies within because I have utilized what are called accelerated learning techniques. At the end of each chapter I have a simple challenge for you to complete and as you finish them one by one you'll be practicing and applying everything you have learned. Doing the exercises will ensure you get the most out of this book and more importantly ensure you improve your athletic ability, so make a promise to me and to yourself to *complete the challenges*!

THE ZEN PERFORMANCE MODEL

*Ever since I was a child I have had this instinctive
urge for expansion and growth. To me, the function
and duty of a quality human being is the sincere and
honest development of one's potential.*
—Bruce Lee

UNDERSTANDING ZEN

"I'm going to try it," said Brannigan one of my favorite students at the high cascade snowboard camp at Snow Park in New Zealand. He was about to attempt a switch front board 270 out and I had full faith he could do it since he was training harder than anyone. The class and coaches all watched as he confidently rode towards the rail, hopped on, and did it flawlessly on the first try. "Yeah!" I yelled, as everyone followed suit in congratulating him.

I wanted everyone at my camp to not only have a good time but also to learn a ton of new snowboard tricks, I mean after all that's why you attend a snowboard camp, right? Michael learned 27 new tricks and nearly every other camper was able to learn more than 20 new tricks after only a one-week camp! We made goals at the start of the camp and if campers were just learning boardslides then it counted as a new trick if they were able to step up to the harder rails, so progression of the same trick counted in their scores. By the end of camp everyone was ecstatic with the incredible progression they had all experienced. When they filled out their surveys at the end every camper gave credit to their success to one main factor which was the Zen Performance Model. It is the most concise, effective, and complete guide to extreme sports performance training available. It contains only tried and tested techniques while covering every area of training necessary to become an elite extreme sports athlete.

Zen is the centerpiece of the model because it represents your growth and progression as an athlete and individual. You are constantly evolving and improving your performance as well as training techniques, and the more you master and apply all the outer components the more results you'll get. You can imagine the model as a wheel that creates a spinning force, and each component provides its own contribution to the total amount of energy generated. When you learn to incorporate and eventually master each component of training, the force you create will continue to grow, and you'll receive greater results.

Zen represents being totally present and at one with yourself. When you are completely in the zone and everything is happening perfectly and naturally, you are experiencing Zen in its truest sense. Zen also means self-expression, growth, and understanding. My intention is for you to train with a Zen mindset, meaning the entire process of training is always done in full awareness and you train effectively, naturally, and efficiently causing you to experience a great deal of self-development, growth, and understanding in the process.

Surrounding the Zen center of the model are the eight other necessary components of Zen Athlete training: visualization, meditation, simulation, nutrition and fitness, confidence, planning and goal setting, dedication, and focus. Each component works in harmony with the next and when you learn to apply and master all of the parts you'll naturally achieve outstanding results. There is a chapter dedicated to each component, and each will be covered in great detail.

If you were to begin mastering each component individually you would quickly notice training one component will help improve another and vice versa. When you are able to gain moderate efficiency in all of the elements you'll begin realizing the full effects of this training model. Remember that it is absolutely imperative that you complete the challenges at the end of each chapter so that you fully understand and internalize the techniques you're learning.

DEDICATION

*We all have dreams. But in order to
make dreams come into reality, it takes an
awful lot of determination, dedication,
self-discipline, and effort.*
—*Jesse Owens*

THE SIMPLE TECHNIQUES FOR HARNESSING THE POWER OF DEDICATION

To be dedicated means that you are committed to your vision; it means you're willing to make sacrifices; it means you want it and you're willing to do what it takes to get it! Lucky for you, dedication should be easy because sports are fun; however, if you're the special kind of athlete who's looking to make some serious progress, dedication to all aspects of your training is essential for your success. The harder you work, the better you'll get; the more committed you are to your training, the more results you'll see. It's that simple.

Extreme sports themselves are such a blast it is understandable that many athletes don't want to put in the extra work to get better, but those who do will experience drastic results. Although going to the gym, dry land training, or sitting and visualizing may not be as much fun as actually going out riding, it's all about perspective. You should treat your chosen sport as an art form; see it as your opportunity to find out what you're capable of. I treat sports like I do martial arts, and that is to develop my mind, body and, in turn, spirit which allows me to become a better martial artist, athlete, and person. The things you will begin to learn when you apply yourself, understand your mind, and do the training will be invaluable to you as you continue through life. Any high level athlete can attest to this.

Although enthusiasm and excitement can get you started this component has one massive hurdle that stops most people dead in their tracks, and that is distraction. The art of distraction control can almost be a component in itself. When pursuing a goal you'll quickly realize it takes hard work to achieve top-notch results and those who are easily distracted will never reach the top of the ladder. Fortunately listed below are several strategies to help you deal with distractions and keep you focused on your goals.

THE THREE TRIED AND TESTED STRATEGIES FOR MASTERING DISTRACTION CONTROL

Plan your Goals

Make monthly, weekly, and daily plans with goals. Lay out a detailed plan for the month and then break it down into four weeks; be sure to make your goals and plans very specific. This way you can monitor how much progress you are making, and you can track your success. Take as many notes as necessary and keep a training journal. Marking down all your successes and failures including what worked and what didn't will help you evolve at a faster pace.

Identify and Record Distractions

As you are going through and recording your progress in your training log, note what your biggest distractions are. Once you can isolate them, come up with a plan to overcome them. For example if you're playing 20 hours of video games a week, spending too much time online, or anything else that is a time waster, then ensure you complete your training before you take part in your distraction. Another

By prevailing over all obstacles and distractions, one may unfailingly arrive at his chosen goal or destination.

—Christopher Columbus

Figure 1.
Planning is your roadmap to success.

very common example of a distraction nowadays is too much time spent on social media like Facebook. You can download apps that monitor your usage so you can see just how much time you're spending and adjust accordingly. Now you must have the discipline to say *no* to them, do what's most important first then reward yourself. Be creative with your solutions, and learn to balance your time and training.

Decide to Commit

Simply deciding that you will commit to something whole-heartedly is very powerful. There is a common denominator between successful people, whether it's sport or business, and that is they have learned the value of hard work. They know that with dedication to an idea, goal, or vision anything is possible and once you decide you are going to stick to something you'll realize you've made a great decision because shortly after the results start coming!

Great minds have told us that success doesn't come from one day's work it comes from days, weeks, months, and years of consistent effort. It is far more beneficial to do a little bit everyday than a whole bunch some days and none on others; commit to being consistent in your training.

Complete This Challenge

Simply just reading about these techniques won't do you a bit of good, so I'd like to offer a simple challenge. Your challenge for the dedication component is to do a minimum of 15 minutes of specific sport training every day for ten days in a row. If you are able to stay committed and do at least one small bit of training every day, whether it's hitting the gym, doing sport-specific cross training, or visualizing, I guarantee at the end of your time you'll notice a substantial improvement. The intention of this exercise is for you to understand the real power of consistent training and commitment; you will soon come to realize that anything is possible with passion and commitment. The world is yours to take, just decide what you want, don't make excuses, and get off your butt, and get it! In your training journal or log make ten circles or boxes. Every day that you train put a giant checkmark in the box, and try and get to all ten without missing a day. Once you are two or three days in, you'll be more motivated to keep your streak going.

FOCUS

One reason so few of us achieve what we truly want is that we never direct our focus; we never concentrate our power. Most people dabble their way through life, never deciding to master anything in particular.
—*Tony Robbins*

THE BLUEPRINT FOR MASTERING FOCUS TO BECOME AN ELITE-LEVEL ATHLETE

Focus means to be fully immersed in the moment giving it your full attention and best effort. Focus is paramount since you will need to learn how to focus on the positive, focus on the moment, focus on your tricks, focus on your training; essentially you'll have to cultivate the ability to have supreme focus in every area of your sport and training. Focus is extremely easy when I'm shredding pow on auto-pilot in the Whistler backcountry, but it gets difficult at times when I need to apply that same focus to my training. It is of great value to learn to stay in the moment, to give your best in each instant and finally to develop specific refocusing plans that will help bring you back to the moment after you've lost it.

Since the ability to apply strong focus can mean the difference between learning to land basic tricks and tricks that are only landed by elite athletes, clearly it's a skill that should be mastered. As you continue to read the words on this page and come to understand how powerful focus really is you might even get excited because you're about to learn an easy way to understand, apply, and develop incredibly powerful focus for your sport.

Get Clear on Your Big Picture

Ask most experts and they'll tell you that you should have a clear vision of your big goal or dream, whether it's winning a contest, getting sponsored, or becoming a pro. It's important to know what you truly want because too many people are focused on going pro when in actuality all you want to do is practice your sport every day. Whatever your goal is be clear on why you want it. You might even change your perspective slightly to say that your focus is to express yourself through sport while developing your mind and body rather than worrying so much about getting paid to do it. Stressing about contests and sponsorships can ruin sport for some people. With the new perspective you don't have to worry about being the best, which allows you to keep practicing your sport from a genuine, fun, and organic place while at the same time developing epic skill.

Break it Down into Manageable Chunks

Now it's time to get clear on the small steps and the habits you'll need to adopt to achieve that big picture goal. Once these habits and necessary action steps are clearly defined you're going to apply laser-like focus to all of these tasks. Learn to focus completely on your training. If you are running on a treadmill learn to run and stop the internal chatter. If you're dry land training pretend you're actually on the hill. If you're on a trampoline be focused there also. The point here is that focus is easy at times when things are fun and exciting and difficult when things are boring or repetitive. The ability to fully focus on the boring or repetitive stuff is an invaluable skill you have to acquire to fully understand the benefits, but I can assure you they are worth the effort!

DISCOVER WHY A REFOCUSING STRATEGY IS ESSENTIAL TO YOUR PROGRESSION

The crowd cheers as they call your name with cameras all around, waiting for you to drop in and you're... distracted. Having to perform at your highest level on command can be a difficult task for some people and learning to focus in practice is the first step to overcoming that. This isn't just reserved for competitions either; this could be when you're filming with your friends or even learning that next big trick. Lack of focus could mean the difference between continuing your progression and taking a trip to the hospital. You should be fully present in your training as mentioned and when you begin to get sidetracked mentally you need some strategies to bring yourself back. There are many different ways you can do this, and most people find intention setting and body awareness or a combination of the two to be the most effective.

The Power of Intention Setting and Programming

Since your mind is infinitely powerful and it responds to your internal dialogue (what you say to yourself), you simply need to direct your conscious and unconscious mind back to the present moment with a reprogramming statement. Here are a couple of examples:

- "It is my intention to be fully aware during this training."
- "I have decided to direct my mind to come back to full awareness of this moment."
- "I am focused and alert; I am fully present."
- "I am fully focused here and now and have decided to land this trick."

You can say whatever you'd like because all that really matters is that you set the intention for your mind to come back. Since your unconscious mind responds to your conscious suggestions simply decide what it is that you'd like to have happen, and make a verbal intention to achieve it.

Breath is the bridge which connects life to consciousness, which unites your body to your thoughts. Whenever your mind becomes scattered, use your breath as the means to take hold of your mind again.

–Thich Nhat Hanh

Conscious Breathing and Body Awareness

As soon as you notice you are losing focus simply begin to become aware of your breathing, pay attention as your breath goes in and out. Focus your attention on the way your body feels, and try and remain fully immersed in the energy and attention of your breathing and body. Your mind will begin to wander, and when it does

Figure 2.
Find your center.

simply bring your awareness back to your breathing or concentrate on feeling your body. Anytime you lose focus from now on STOP, and take three deep breaths in and out through your nose, and you'll come back to full awareness.

Combination

There are no strict rules on how to influence your own mind, only guidelines. The most successful way for developing a strong mental focus for most athletes has come from combining the two techniques of intention setting and body awareness. Simply take in three deep breaths trying to focus completely on your breathing while repeating a simple intention to yourself such as "I am now completely focused." This simple strategy is usually all it takes to become fully focused almost instantly.

HOW TO GET IN THE ZONE ANYTIME, ANYWHERE, QUICKLY, AND EASILY

What is "the zone"? It's a state of pure awareness where you are totally confident. It's a state of mind where you trust yourself completely and everything just flows. Clearly this state of mind would be greatly beneficial as you begin to imagine yourself performing your sport effortlessly, landing all of your tricks with ease and style. The zone is simply the most powerful state of mind you can have while enjoying your sport, your mindset is total confidence and self-belief. Most people only enter the zone on rare occasions because it happens naturally as a result of a few good runs and a positive thought process; however, there is a way that you can enter the zone at will by using what's called a trigger in NLP terms.

A trigger is any external stimulus that creates an internal response. A famous example of this is the study by Ivan Pavlov (1910) on dogs. Researchers rang a bell when it was time for the dogs to eat, and after a few short days when the researchers rang the bell, regardless of whether it was time to eat, the dogs would begin salivating. Your mind works in the same manner, meaning you can use your thoughts to create internal responses that will force you into the zone or a state of massive confidence. The good news is that the process is really quite simple.

THE FOUR KEY PRINCIPLES FOR GETTING INTO THE ZONE

Make the Decision

Decide that you want to be in the zone and set the intention to get in the zone with an affirmation of some kind.

- "I am in the zone."
- "I love the thought of being in the zone."
- "I've decided I'm going to get in the zone and perform my best."
- "I'm going to perform my best."

The sentence doesn't matter as long as it expresses your goal simply and directly in a way that feels good to you.

Utilize Powerful Memories

Remember a time when you were in the zone or had total and complete confidence in yourself. I use the time when I made 24 free throws in a row, and then concentrate on how I felt, and make the memory as real as possible, and focus on the feeling of confidence.

STOP! Right now at this very moment I want you to begin searching your memory banks for a time when you were playing a sport or doing anything where you had total and complete confidence.

Now that you have chosen a memory, replay it in your mind making it as real as possible, and focus on the feelings of confidence and

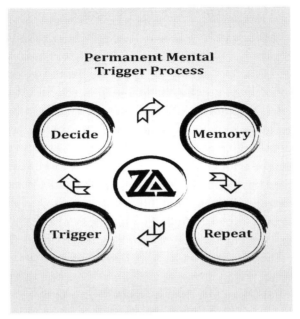

Figure 3.
This is a simple process to hardwire confidence in the
body. The more you do the process the more neural
networks will be created in the brain.

being in the zone. The memory doesn't necessarily have to relate to
your sport. The most important part of this step is to remember a
time you felt the most self-confidence and ability.

Burn it into Your Mind with a Trigger

The next step as you continue to focus on the memory of being in
the zone is setting your trigger. In this step you need to visualize this
memory in as much detail as possible a minimum of five times, but
the more the better. Each time you replay the confident memory in
your mind, try and make the feeling of confidence double. You can
also mentally add epic music in the background of your visualization

that will help get you pumped up. It could be something like the *Rocky* soundtrack. It may seem silly, but it works.

Now when you replay the memory in your mind and feel the confidence build to its pinnacle squeeze your left fist and repeat internally or out loud: "I am in the zone. I am fully confident. I will perform my best." You can use any sentence that instills confidence.

Continue to visualize this memory a minimum of five times, and each time try and double the feeling of confidence, and squeeze your left fist at the pinnacle of each visualization.

Triple the Power by Repeating the Process

Now when you are engaged in your sport you can use the trigger as necessary by simply squeezing your left fist and saying, "I am in the zone." If done correctly, this trigger should instantly alter your state of mind and increase your confidence and concentration. Remember the more feeling you can put into your visualizations the more it will take effect when you squeeze your fist and set the trigger. If your trigger has no effect on the hill simply keep repeating the steps until it does, the more times you visualize and strengthen the trigger the more effect it will have.

A powerful and effective trigger will take 10 to 30 rounds of practice to take effect. They don't have to be all at once, but it is good practice to strengthen your trigger daily until you feel it's as strong as possible. This process can take some time since you are building new neural pathways in the brain; repetition is required to have effect, so be patient.

THE FAIL SAFE METHOD TO STOMPING TRICKS AFTER FALLING

If you're learning new tricks then you're probably going to eat it every now and again; it's just a part of the game. The real trick is learning to mentally recover and land the trick the next time around. After a fall many athletes will begin to get into a very negative mindset and become afraid of the trick and fall repeatedly as their confidence is gradually shattered into nothing. There is a straightforward and potent strategy you can use to stomp tricks after hard bails. This process should be used every time you fall, furthermore if you don't land it perfectly you can use this strategy to help learn and perfect the trick much sooner.

The chances are, if you're like most athletes, you're making a major mistake without even realizing it. Falling is a part of all sports and most athletes don't deal with it properly. The absolute worst thing that you can do after falling is to over think it and dwell upon what just happened. You have to develop a very short memory and make sure that you're seeing yourself land that trick and keeping your internal dialogue positive despite failure. So many times I'll see athletes psych themselves out and risk an even greater injury. If you're freaked out about the trick you can give it a break or try something smaller until you build up the confidence to try and land it once again. You must try tricks with complete confidence, and if you can't you must build up to it.

Don't dwell on what went wrong. Instead focus on what to do next. Spend your energies on moving forward towards finding the answer.

–Denis Waitley

Visualize in Reverse

The first thing you're going to do after you've fallen is visualize the trick you just tried in your mind and mentally replay your fall three times backwards starting with the end of the fall and ending with the approach.

Visualize the Trick Perfectly Disassociated

After mentally replaying the image in reverse, run the mental tape forward and visualize yourself completing the trick exactly how you wanted. Do this three times making the visualizations as real as possible. Focus on making the images in your mind big, bright, and clear. Some people pretend they are front and center at a massive movie theatre in their mind and put their intended visualizations on the big screen.

Visualize the Trick Perfectly Associated

The third step is to visualize yourself completing the trick exactly as you intended three more times from approach to landing, and this time focus on the *feeling* of landing the trick, performance, or run. Feel the approach, feel yourself going through the motions of the trick, and finally feel the sense of excitement you'll feel when you land the trick and all that happiness that goes along with landing tricks.

Set Your Powerful Intention and Keep the Self-Talk Positive

The final step is to mentally set a positive intention by telling yourself:

- "This trick is easy."
- "I will land this trick every time."
- "I can land this trick."

Any positively worded statement will work, follow this process every time you fall and you'll be certain to land a significantly higher number of your next attempts. If you fall again simply repeat the process. The second you allow a trick to mentally beat you, you're done, and you won't land the trick until you can overcome the fear.

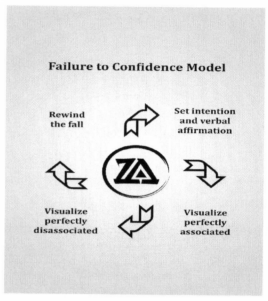

Figure 4.
This process helps hardwire the desired result into the mind and body.

It is of paramount importance that you choose to focus on the positive in all situations in sport and life. The more aware and present you are for the little things the more you'll experience joy, relaxation, and success in your life. The entire Buddhist and Zen philosophies rely mostly on the ability to stay present in the moment. Begin by applying specific focus to your training; don't simply go through the motions, be fully present, and give 100 percent every time. Although this is a very simple concept it can be extremely difficult to do, and the select few who dedicate themselves to cultivating the ability of supreme focus through consistent practice and refocus will experience benefits that go far beyond exceptional athletic skill.

Complete This Challenge

The challenge for the focus component is very simple, and it's in two parts. The first part is for you to practice using the zone trigger technique and follow the process at least five times. To go one step further, for those of you who want to master this technique and see the benefits instantly, all you need to do is follow the process five times a day for the next five days, and whenever you use that zone trigger you'll be flooded with an overwhelming feeling of confidence. The second part of this challenge is to try and show increased focus and concentration in more areas of your life and training, for example when you are training, walking somewhere, eating, or doing anything else that requires focus. Rather than letting your mind wander try to keep a state of comfortable awareness, and when you find yourself unfocused use a refocus plan to come back to full awareness.

MEDITATION

Meditation brings wisdom; lack of meditation leaves ignorance. Know well what leads you forward and what holds you back, and choose the path that leads to wisdom
—Hindu Prince Gautama Siddhar

UNLOCK THE SECRET POWER OF MEDITATION TO MAKE THE IMPOSSIBLE POSSIBLE

Have you ever wondered if you are really in control of your mind? Most people are confused, stressed, depressed, hypnotized, and the worst part is that they don't even notice they are on autopilot or know why they feel so bad. These states of mind are really tough to avoid since we are all under constant mental attack through television, radio, Internet, billboards, schools, peers, and authority figures. Breaking the cycle and learning to think independently from all external stimulus and persuasion is no easy task.

The ability to have complete control of your thoughts, access to universal intelligence, and a bridge to realizing your full potential is what meditation is really about. Cultivating these skills is not only essential for your athletic progression it is critical for your development as a human being. The extreme circus that is life with all the grand experiences both good and bad separate us as individuals; however, we have one major common denominator, that is we all live and die, and everything in between is our own interpretation of what we have experienced.

We are on this planet to learn, discover, and know ourselves, and from that we acquire true wisdom and understanding. The more you know yourself the more your inner strength, confidence, and intuition grow. Hence meditation changes your reality and daily experience of living. Meditation is the equivalent to taking the most potent steroids for your mind that will produce clarity, self-confidence, and purpose. When you work out your body it responds, as does the mind, to proper training. Meditation will improve your abilities a great deal. Many great athletes such as Michael Jordan, Bruce Lee, Jack Nicholas, and countless others are known advocates and give much credit for their success to the mental game and meditation. Here are just a few proven benefits to meditation.

General benefits:

- Improved focus
- Increased confidence
- Improved concentration
- Improved health
- Improved learning and better retention of information
- More likely to achieve goals
- Deeper understanding of yourself
- Reduced anxiety and stress
- Experience more positive emotions such as relaxation, joy, excitement, and happiness

Sport-specific benefits:

- Improved ability to get in and stay in the zone
- Improved ability to concentrate on tricks and runs easier (higher percentage of landing versus falling rates)
- Improved ability to relax more through competition, ultimately improving performance
- Increased effectiveness of visualizations
- Better understanding and monitoring of your internal dialogue

Science has proven meditation is incredibly beneficial to the mind and body, which most people have no problem believing; however, it goes much deeper than that *(Santarnecchi et al., 2014)*. The practice of meditation will have a more powerful and positive impact on your life than winning a million dollars. That's a bold statement I know, but what is learned and experienced by looking within can never be purchased with currency.

The problem is that many people want to try meditating but don't because they're unclear on how to meditate or claim not to have enough time. This chapter is not to tell you the history of meditation or why it works. The aim is to teach you how to meditate and help you get started. When you begin seeing the benefits and add meditation to your daily routine you'll find yourself experiencing a much better existence on this planet because you'll know, understand, and accept yourself; you'll connect with the unified field, unconscious or universal intelligence; and you'll develop an unshakable confidence in yourself as you continue to deliberately create the experiences you would like to have. Meditation will have a profound effect on your athletic ability and training. Seriously!

What is Meditation?

Oddly enough there is no one widespread accepted definition of meditation. This is perfect because it is different for everyone and there is no right or wrong way (for the most part) to meditate. Meditation is merely self-reflection, contemplation, the practice of stilling the mind, observing thought, reflection, or any other way you want to describe sitting still, looking within, and quieting the mind.

The Essential Principles of Meditation Practice

- Find somewhere quiet where you will not be disturbed.
- Wear comfortable clothes.
- Sit comfortably on a chair or on the floor on a cushion with your legs crossed and hands placed wherever comfortable. You can lie on the floor or in your bed, and if you find yourself falling asleep, change your position to sitting.
- Keep your back straight, and your tongue on the roof of your mouth.
- Breathe in through your nose deeply using your diaphragm or belly. Breathe out through your nose.
- Get to it!

FOUR SURPRISINGLY SIMPLE AND POWERFUL MEDITATIONS

There are many ways you can meditate with no right or wrong. Below are four quick and easy ways you can start your meditation practice today.

Guided Meditation

Go to a bookstore, search YouTube, or even make one yourself (you'll learn how in a later chapter). Simply find a guided meditation and sit and listen. This is an excellent way to experience your first couple of meditations.

Breathing Meditation

Sit in a quiet place and take slow deep breaths in and out through your nose. When thoughts arise, and they will, acknowledge them, then release them, and bring your focus back to your breathing. That's it. Remember keep it simple because it is. You can practice counting your breaths if that helps. Thoughts will bombard you during your first few sessions, but eventually you'll have pleasant gaps of time where you are simply breathing with absolutely nothing going on in your head, and that's the point! The longer you practice meditation, the gaps of time of pure relaxation and no thought will increase; however it does take some work. You can download relaxing music to help. Search for meditation music or relaxing music; personally I enjoy Tibetan singing bowls.

Mantra Meditation

A mantra meditation is when you repeat a word or phrase to yourself. To give this technique a try simply decide on a word or a phrase that you will repeat either silently in your head or out loud for the duration of your meditation. Repeat this mantra over and over trying to keep your focus on the word or phrase. Here are some examples of mantras

- Peace
- Focus
- Concentration
- Confidence
- Now
- Love
- Inspiration
- Inner peace
- I am confident
- I am calm
- I feel peace

To understand the immeasurable, the mind must be extraordinarily quiet, still.

—Jiddu Krishnamurti

You can use any word or phrase that you like. The purpose is to meditate on that phrase with full concentration, just like the breathing meditation, and after a little bit of practice you'll begin experiencing very pleasant gaps in internal mental chatter. The more you can create these gaps and focus on your mantra the more you'll begin to see and understand the benefits of meditation practice.

Daily Mindfulness Meditation

Meditation is really anything where you apply full focus without thinking of anything else. If you are walking somewhere and you try to be fully in the present moment feeling your feet beneath you, listening to all the sounds intently, and trying to maintain full awareness, that is a meditation. You can do it while cooking, cleaning, folding laundry, or any other mundane tasks. Practice meditation simply by being as in the moment as possible. As you are completing your tasks and notice your mind begin to wander simply gently bring your attention back to the present moment and experience. Many people love extreme sports or activities that gives them no choice but to focus. You feel free and at ease when you are doing these activities because you are fully present and experiencing the moment without conscious thought. Here are a few examples of this type of meditation you may enjoy.

- Walking meditation
- Sun gazing
- Surfing
- Driving
- Eating

Zen masters often teach their students that there are many levels of learning, understanding, knowledge, and wisdom. My intention in this chapter, and in this book for that matter, is to use words that will cause a physical response to the practices because simply reading this will do very little for you. True knowledge and understanding will come when you acquire the willpower to perform these exercises. It is my sincerest hope that if nothing else is taken from this book you are one of the few who are able to commit to the daily practice of meditation, at first you won't understand why, but with a little dedication and after a few short weeks of application you will begin to develop a level of understanding and begin experiencing the many extraordinary benefits of meditation.

Do not mistake the simplicity of this task for its effectiveness, most people try and meditate for too long at first so they never do it. Simply meditate for one minute on your first day, and add an additional minute every day until you get to ten minutes. Once you have adopted the practice of meditation, even just five minutes of meditation can have a profound impact on your day and subsequently your life. Remember the most important thing about meditation is to keep it simple, focus on your breathing while gently trying to clear your mind. Eventually you will begin to have gaps of clear mindedness or, in Zen, "no mind" that will grow more and more with each meditation.

10 Day Meditation Guide		
DAY	**TIME**	**COMPLETED**
1	Meditate for one minute, yes one minute	☑
2	2	☐
3	3	☐
4	4	☐
5	5	☐
6	6	☐
7	7 +	☐
8	8 +	☐
9	9 +	☐
10	10 +	☐

Figure 5.
The most effective way to begin a meditation practice is to simply meditate for one minute on your first day, and add an additional minute every day until you get to ten minutes.

Complete This Challenge

The challenge you face in learning the meditation component of Zen is to complete this challenge and discover how to clear your mind on command. Do not try to attain anything during meditation, and don't worry whether you're doing it right. If you're trying to sit in silence and thoughts keep coming up then you're doing it right. It takes some practice before you can get that beautiful inner silence. Don't worry, you'll get there. Keep the practice very simple and in the repeated action you will gain understanding.

Following the steps outlined in the chapter is a foolproof way for you to adopt the habit of meditation as a part of your lifestyle. The key is to meditate daily without missing a day.

VISUALIZATION

Before every shot, I go to the movies.
—Jack Nicklaus

USING VISUALIZATION TO GET RESULTS

You are about to discover a common thread that links all great athletes together. It is widely believed that your inner world creates your outer reality. Whatever you see in your mind will eventually be manifested if given enough focus and belief. Constantly visualizing your tricks will program your mind and body to be able to perform those actions. Daily visualization and positive internal dialogue are essential to fast progression and can take you far beyond what you thought possible when you commit to the practice. It is imperative you learn to add visualization to your training because it works, furthermore it is probably the most effective training you can do. To cite one excellent example, Australian psychologist Alan Richardson (1967) conducted a visualization experiment involving students shooting basketball free throws. He divided them into three groups. Group A practiced shooting free throws every day for 20 days. Group B shot free throws on the 1st and 20th day. Group C shot free throws on the 1st day and 20th day and in addition, they spent 20 minutes per day visualizing making free throws.

On the 20th day Richardson measured the results. Group A improved by 24%, Group B had no improvement, while Group C improved by 23%, nearly as much as the subjects who practiced shooting daily by simply visualizing sinking the shot. This is one of many studies that prove that visualization not only works, it works exceptionally well!

You're about to learn a blueprint for programming and reprogramming the mind to the point where your subconscious mind takes over and literally forces you to create the beliefs, circumstances, and experiences necessary to realize your goals in sport and life. You might be thinking to yourself that this is too good to be true so allow me to give you some proof.

The Experiment	
Group A	Instructed to practice shooting free throws every day for 20 days
Group B	Instructed to shoot free throws on the 1st day and 20th day
Group C	Instructed to shoot free throws on the 1st day and 20th day. They also spent 20 minutes per day visualizing free throws.
The results	
Group A	Improved by 24 percent
Group B	No Improvement
Group C	Improved by 23 percent

I train myself mentally with visualization. The morning of a tournament, before I put my feet on the floor, I visualize myself making perfect runs with emphasis on technique, all the way through to what my personal best is in practice.... The more you work with this type of visualization, especially when you do it on a day-to-day basis, you'll actually begin to feel your muscles contracting at the appropriate times.

—Camille Duvall

The painful truth of the matter is that we as individuals are mostly run by our subconscious beliefs, thoughts, and desires. What makes matters worse is the fact most of us have no idea what beliefs or ideologies we have that could be sabotaging us. Often we are influenced without even knowing it; however, we have the power to craft our minds and our internal belief system, and this has truly remarkable power. In many parts of our lives there is a great deal of importance placed on the levels of the mind including psychology, advertising, teaching, training, therapy, law and security, politics, and so much more. The fact is that our subconscious can be persuaded and manipulated quite easily by external stimulus; however, the best news is that once we know how we can create anything we desire.

According to research, using brain imagery and visualization is effective because neurons in our brains transmit information and interpret imagery as equivalent to a real-life action (Morris, Spittle, Watt, 2005). Put another way, your mind thinks it's real. Visualization is a common practice used among Olympic athletes, even in disciplines such as track and field and weight lifting, and has proven to increase performance. When we visualize an act, the brain generates an impulse that tells our neurons to execute the movement. This creates or enhances an existing neural pathway (a group of cells in our brain that work together to create memories or learned behaviors) and prepares our body to act in a way consistent to what we imagined. All of this occurs without actually performing the physical activity, yet it achieves a similar result (Morris, Spittle, Watt, 2005).

Many schools of thought break visualization into two categories. The first being outcome visualization where you visualize yourself living the outcome you desire. For you, this could mean seeing yourself playing your sport every day with a ton of sponsors. The second type is process visualization where you see yourself take all the necessary steps to achieve your outcome.

HOW TO UNLEASH THE POWER OF VISUALIZATION

Associated Visualization

Associated visualization, otherwise known as first person visualization, is when you visualize as if you're seeing the action through your own eyes exactly as you do in daily life (O'Connor, 2001). During this visualization it is very important to focus on the *feeling* of the trick and your body. Feel your equipment, whether board, bike, or anything else, feel the wind on your face, feel your body as it goes through the motions, and be as detailed as possible. Do your best to imagine in great detail every part of the maneuver. When you end this visualization a very powerful additional tool is to feel the joy, excitement, and happiness that goes with landing the trick perfectly, this will give your unconscious mind more fuel to remember the trick, and do it again.

Disassociated Visualization

Disassociated visualization is when you utilize a third person viewpoint (O'Connor, 2001). This means you are looking at yourself from an outside perspective, as if you were on TV or you were a different person watching the action. You can imagine yourself on an IMAX big screen and watch yourself perform the trick in perfect detail from any angle you like, above, below, the side. Make sure you see exactly what your body needs to do to perform the trick

Figure 7.
Make your mind movie as real as possible, your brain and body don't know the difference!

THE THREE FUNDAMENTALS FOR SHOCKINGLY EFFECTIVE VISUALIZATIONS

Include All Five Senses.

You are essentially hardwiring your mind and body together during a visualization and adding sight, sound, taste, touch, and smell to convince your brain it's real. The goal is to make the visualizations as authentic as possible. Play around with your senses when you're visualizing and practice focusing in on each sense until they all become tuned in automatically. The two most important senses are your visual (inner sight) and kinesthetic (inner feeling) senses.

Always Visualize Perfection.

This is self-explanatory, but you may have some problems visualizing tricks you can't do; however, to combat this problem simply remember a time when you saw the trick performed on a video or by someone else, and use that memory to get the flawless images. Every single time you visualize a trick see yourself do it perfectly.

Blow it up and Watch it on the Big Screen

In your mind's eye make the images as *big, bright,* and *clear* as possible. You can pretend you are in the front row in a theatre that has the most epic screen in the entire world and watch yourself perform the tricks you're learning in perfect detail.

You can see how easy the process of visualization is. Remember that all of the processes in this book are extremely powerful and made simple for a reason. Don't make the mistake of thinking they won't work because they are simple. I dare you to apply these techniques and take your sport to the next level.

THE SECRET PRE-TRICK VISUALIZATION FORMULA

If there was a way you could increase the likelihood of landing your tricks by 50 to 75 percent, would you want to know how? You are now aware of the power of visualization, both associated and disassociated, how to perform it effectively, and different ways in which you can visualize, so clearly you're ready for mas-

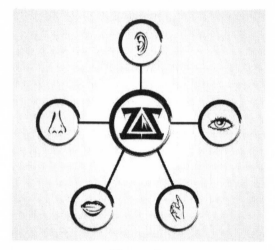

Figure 8.
The more real you make the visualization the more effective it will be.

tery. Combination visualization is a little known formula I developed to help top athletes perform their best. The athletes who perform this process *every single time* before attempting a trick notice themselves landing tricks faster, falling less, having better style, and progressing quicker.

Start by clearing your mind. The easiest way to do this is to take three deep breaths in and out through your nose. If you already have a technique that allows you to clear your mind quickly feel free to use that instead; however, conscious breathing is a surefire way for you to quiet the mind and connect with yourself.

Once your mind is clear, visualize yourself performing the trick from both the first and third person at once. This time try and focus on bringing in all five senses. Focus on amplifying all of the feelings, images, and sounds that you're experiencing in your visualization. This round will be easier because you've already done it once, and as you increase the intensity of the visualization the process becomes more effective.

HOW TO SUPER CHARGE THE VISUALIZATION PROCESS

The effects the visualization process will have on your performance are going to be profound; however, there is a simple way to give even more power to your visualization by adding two simple elements: set the intention of confidence and create positive internal dialogue.

The first element is to set the intention or decide to double the feeling of confidence. Before each visualization you can set the intention and plainly direct your mind to make the visualization much clearer, to double your feelings of self-belief and confidence as you watch your mental movie. Simply direct your mind to increase the effectiveness and clarity before each visualization.

The second element is an affirmation or positive internal dialogue statement before you attempt your trick and after the visualization process. For example some of the things I often tell myself (which may not necessarily be true) include:

- "This trick is easy. I'm going to land it."
- "I love the thought of landing this line perfectly."
- "I can do this trick."
- "I will do (X)."

Say whatever feels right, all you need to do is set that intention and mentally repeat that statement in your mind after your visualization to increase impact. After you've completed the visualization process and repeated a positive statement you can drop in with absolute confidence!

Mental Training Tip

If you perform the trick or maneuver perfectly, replay the success in your mind. If you didn't land the trick or you didn't do it absolutely perfectly it is important to pretend you did, and go through the trick in your mind and visualize it the way you wanted it to go. This will continue to hardwire the trick into your mind. Eventually you will learn the trick, then you'll land it on command, and you won't need to visualize it unless you're stepping up to a more difficult feature because performing the trick will become automatic, and it'll be rooted deep within your mind and body.

HOW TO MAKE OUTRAGEOUSLY EFFECTIVE GUIDED VISUALIZATIONS

In this section you're going to learn how to create extremely powerful and customized guided visualizations that are going to help you to maintain a fast and continual progression. Every single day more and more proof is coming to light about how powerful visualization is, and that's just the beginning. When you begin the daily practice of visualization you'll begin to experience greater benefits that will shock you.

The greatest basketball player of all time Michael Jordan used meditation and visualization in practice and before games (Jackson, 2013). Olympic gymnasts, ski racers, jumpers, and countless other top athletes spend massive amounts of time mentally rehearsing their sports; obviously you should too. The process in which you can complete this task is extremely simple, and you can do it in one of two ways or both, if you so desire.

The process of relaxing yourself and accessing your unconscious mind has many great benefits. Most people are unaware that your unconscious mind doesn't know the difference between something real or imagined (visualized), which means you can seemingly hardwire new beliefs, skills, or habits with relative ease. It is important to know that there are levels to the mind, which have different functions and abilities. The conscious mind is responsible for short term memory and rational thinking. It has a limited processing capacity and limited space. The critical factor is the gatekeeper to the subconscious. It is the rational processing and comparison between reality and subconscious belief systems (O'Connor and McDermott, 1996).

Next we have the subconscious mind, which has unlimited space, holds beliefs about the self and the world, is responsible for thoughts, habits and emotions, and is programmable through suggestion and visualization. The deepest layer of the mind is the unconscious mind, which looks after our immune system, autonomic nervous system, and automatic body functions such as regulating the heart and lungs (O'Connor and McDermott, 1996).

Now that you have an understanding of the layers of the mind, you surely realize that to make real change you need to access the subconscious mind. You are now ready to learn some techniques that will grant you access to the unconscious mind while being armed with the most effective tools for programming yourself to achieve your goals.

Free Associated Visualization

Wouldn't it be amazing if we could harness the power of the subconscious easily? The truth is that everyone has the ability to access the deeper parts of the mind, and it's truly quite simple to do. Begin by quieting your mind and then simply play with your imagination allowing yourself to visualize and experience all the things that you're trying to learn or accomplish. Free associated visualization is simply the process of first relaxing yourself completely allowing access to the subconscious mind and then daydreaming, visualizing, and imagining your goals.

The easiest way to get started is to take in ten deep breaths and focus completely on your breathing. Set the intention for your mind to relax and focus on easy, slow, and deep breaths. By the time you get to ten you'll be quite relaxed and ready for the second step. If you have your own process for clearing your mind then you can certainly use that method instead. Once you are in a relaxed state begin to visualize whatever tricks you're trying to learn in crystal clear detail. Have fun experiencing this calm state of mind while you imagine yourself accomplishing all of the goals you've set out for yourself. Many of the athletes I've worked with find it's best to pick out one to three tricks maximum for the free associated visualization to maintain better focus rather than trying to do too much at once. Other athletes prefer to continually review a particular move they are trying to nail down. It is important to realize that there is no right or wrong way to do this, and the more you practice the more confident you'll be that you're doing it right.

Self-Guided Visualizations

Self-guided visualizations differ from free associated visualizations because you will record and narrate the visualizations. The main problems with self-guided visualizations are that most athletes don't realize how influential guided visualizations truly are and those who

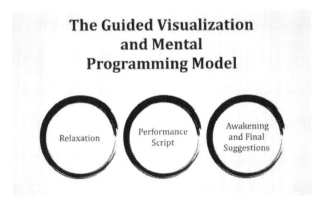

Figure 9.
Making guided visualizations is as simple as 1, 2, 3.

do don't know how to make them. The truth is they are so easy to make a first grader could do it. There are limitless options with this type of method, for example you could make a recording for one specific trick or you could make a guided visualization of an upcoming contest or environment you know you'll need to perform in. You can be as creative as you want and make your visualizations as long or short as you want. The best part is there really isn't a wrong way to do it; however, there are ways that work better than others and in less than two minutes you're going to know exactly how!

What You'll Need:

- Something that records audio
- A script
- A quiet place to record
- A quiet place to listen

Remember to keep this process simple. All you need to do is get a recording device and write a script that includes the relaxation technique, the trick description, and the final suggestion. You can use your phone, computer, or any other recording device. As your brain allows the information in the script to process, you will come to realize you can apply visualization easily. When you complete the visualization challenge you'll be excited to know that you have acquired the skill of visualization to use for the rest of your life.

Part 1: Empty Your Mind

The first step in the process is to clear your mind. The key is to stop your internal dialogue which will allow you to reach your subconscious mind and allow the visualizations and suggestions to be effective. Quieting the mind is an art in itself and there is more than one way to accomplish this. Most experts highly recommend the practice of meditation to anyone hoping to be a top athlete regardless of the sport. While meditation and stilling the mind can be a difficult task I have provided you with three astoundingly easy ways to clear your mind and completely relax.

The Power of Your Breath. Focus on your breathing for ten or more breaths. Guide yourself to relax as much as possible. Simply talk yourself into a deep state of relaxation by merely suggesting it. Here is an example of a script to guide you to relaxation.

> Take in a deep breath in through your nose, and exhale slowly allowing yourself to relax completely. Take in another deep breath, trying to relax yourself as much as possible.

Continue to walk yourself through ten deep breaths while repeating the suggestion to *relax deeply*.

The Countdown Method. This is virtually the same technique as above except you countdown from ten to one while suggesting you relax deeper and deeper. Here is an example of a script you can use.

> Relax your body as much as possible, I am going to countdown from ten to one, and with each count you will allow yourself to relax deeper and deeper. Ten ... relaxing your mind and body. Nine ... allowing yourself to relax deeper. Eight ... completely relaxed letting go of all your thoughts. Seven ... even deeper now. Six ... completely letting go of all your worries. Five ... feeling a deep sense of relaxation from the top of your head

to the tip of your toes. Four … even deeper now feeling completely relaxed. Three … completely relaxed. Two … double the feeling of relaxation you are experiencing, and when I count to one you'll allow yourself to relax as deeply as possible. And one … completely relaxed, completely at ease.

It doesn't have to be those exact words because you're simply helping yourself relax. Don't complicate it; just try it.

The Rapid Speed Induction. This is a quick and easy relaxation process where you guide yourself through three deep breaths, and then you clench your fists and give yourself the suggestion to double the feeling of relaxation. Let me explain further. As you inhale for each breath clench your hands and tense your arms, and when you exhale relax your hands and arms while trying to relax yourself as deeply as possible. Here is a sample script.

Take a deep breath in through your nose and exhale slowly allowing yourself to relax deeply. Now make a fist with your hands and squeeze tightly, and when you let go you will double the feeling of relaxation and completely relax. Squeeze your fists now, and hold for five seconds, then release them allowing yourself to double the feeling of relaxation. Squeeze your fists again, and hold for three seconds. Release your hands and double the feeling of relaxation once again. Now squeeze your fists one last time for three seconds, and allow yourself to relax as deeply as possible.

In NLP or hypnotherapy terms, this is the tension/relaxation technique followed by a command suggestion. The point here is to relax yourself as quickly as possible because the deeper you go and the more still your mind, the better the visualizations will work.

Mental Training Tip

The key is to use your own breathing to relax yourself and use the suggestions and relaxation scripts for assistance. When you are listening to your guided visualizations direct your unconscious mind to completely relax by simply giving it a command such as, "My intention is to completely relax; I am allowing myself to completely relax from my head to my toes," or anything else you'd like to tell yourself. Finally when you read your scripts you don't need a special voice, simply use your own natural voice and speak slowly and clearly.

Part 2: The Performance Script

Now that your mind is in a relaxed state you can begin narrating the script you've made that describes in detail the tricks you are learning. This part is particularly simple because all you need to do is write down a description of the tricks you want to learn. If you were a snowboarder creating a guided visualization for a 360 it might sound something like this.

See yourself waiting to hit the jump, and now you're ready to drop in. You're confidently approaching the jump, and you're initiating your set up turn. Now you're at the bottom of the jump and you're slowly transferring your weight to your heel edge getting ready for the frontside 360. You're going up the jump in perfect balance with equal weight on both feet; your body is slightly counter-rotated ready for the spin. You're at the lip of the jump now, and you've released into the spin perfectly. You're now in the air and the spin has begun....

The important thing is to simply describe performing the tricks in as much detail as possible. It may seem a bit awkward at first and when you begin to listen to your audios it will get much easier and you'll begin to learn what to say and how to describe the trick to yourself to get the clearest and easiest images to follow along with.

Part 3: Final Suggestions and Awakening

There are many myths surrounding hypnosis and guided meditations that suggest a person can be stuck in that state, but the truth is that if you make yourself a guided meditation or visualization the worst thing that could happen is you could fall asleep or stay nice and peacefully relaxed for longer than you planned to. It's a very effective and powerful practice to make suggestions or commands at the end of your audios. These are called final suggestions. You can make any final command or statement you desire and feel will be most useful to you. Here are a few examples.

- "I can now easily perform all the tricks I have just visualized."
- "My sport is easy and fun. I learn tricks quickly. I am progressing extremely fast."
- "I have a deep belief in my ability. I can learn any trick quickly."

The last part of the recording is designed to bring you back to a wakeful, alert, and positive frame of mind. You can use the following script as a guideline and again there is no right or wrong wording; simply narrate your intention.

On the count of three you will awake feeling totally refreshed with fantastic new energy. Three … starting to feel your body. Two … coming back to awareness more and more, and on the count of one you'll open your eyes feeling totally refreshed and vital with happy positive energy. And one … eyes open feeling great and full of energy.

When you open your eyes you should have ideally enjoyed using your imagination to guide you through the procedure of doing the trick or tricks you are trying to learn. This method simply helps guide your imagination to stay focused and allows you to daydream with less distraction and more clarity. As you enjoy listening to each guided visualization your neural pathways will grow and the trick will become hardwired into your mind and body.

The guided visualization model is extremely simple and powerful. The perfect strategy for getting the most out of this technique is to make yourself a guided visualization for the tricks you'd like to learn and listen to them repeatedly. Take your progression in steps, and once you achieve a goal or trick simply make a new audio continuing your progression

Complete This Challenge

You have two challenges for the visualization component. For the first challenge, close your eyes and try to apply the three fundamentals of visualization as you imagine yourself biting into a lemon. In your mind's eye put a big, juicy lemon in your hand. Begin to peel the lemon and as the peel easily comes off notice the smell, and texture of the lemon, and get ready to take a big bite. As your mouth closes around the lemon, feel your teeth bite into the flesh of the lemon as the juices squirt into your mouth. Simply do your best to imagine in as great of detail as possible biting into a big juicy lemon. If you're like most people I'm sure your mouth is watering right now, mine is just by writing about it.

Your second challenge is to make yourself three guided audios for three different tricks you would like to learn that are currently within your abilities. Keep them short and simple, and then listen to them. Once you've listened to all three you'll realize how easy they are to make as well as how fun and effective they are. When you complete this challenge you'll have the ability to make specific brief or extended guided visualizations for your sport and life. This technique can be applied to other sports and life goals with the same degree of success.

BELIEF

A man can be as great as he wants to be. If you believe in yourself and have the courage, the determination, the dedication, the competitive drive, and if you are willing to sacrifice the little things in life and pay the price for the things that are worthwhile, it can be done.
—*Vince Lombardi*

HOW TO UNLEASH YOUR UNLIMITED INNER POWER AND DEVELOP UNSHAKABLE CONFIDENCE AND SELF WORTH

You may not know this, but there is one major factor that has been guiding your life since the day you were born and will continue to be your critical underlying factor until the day you die. This factor will determine how successful you will become, how happy you will be, how hard or easy life will be, and everything else in between. After reading the title of this chapter, you may have guessed that this crucial factor is confidence, and you may become curious about how much of an influence core beliefs really are. What you believe about yourself and what you believe you can accomplish will determine the value and success of your life. The core beliefs we choose to adopt shape our lives, and we search daily for proof to increase the strength of those beliefs. This is a dangerous realization for those of you who have embraced beliefs that are limiting, negative, and detrimental to your development as an athlete and as a person. What's even worse is that most people have a collection of limiting beliefs and don't even realize it. If you were to read this chapter of the book and do the exercises you can breathe a sigh of relief because you're about to uncover what your current beliefs are and furthermore how to reset them so you can achieve your highest potential.

Many great athletes have verbalized that they hold an incredibly strong belief in their ability to achieve greatness, as do countless inventors, entrepreneurs, philanthropists, artists, and leaders. The point of this chapter is not to give you the old fashioned motivational speech that goes something like, "Believe in yourselves, kids, and all your dreams will come true!" The real power in personal development comes from analyzing your current beliefs in sport and life, understanding them, and making the changes necessary to ensure that you have self-serving beliefs that are built on a solid foundation, not merely illusions of the ego. Your beliefs shape your behavior, habits, and decisions, which ultimately determine your level of confidence.

A BLUEPRINT FOR UNCOVERING THE LIMITING BELIEFS THAT ARE HOLDING YOU BACK

Figure 10.
Beliefs are the foundation of your results

Beliefs are the core element to your success in sport and anything you undertake in life. To succeed you must embrace and internalize beliefs that are empowering, positive, encouraging, and most importantly beliefs of possibility and opportunity. You can apply these beliefs to sport and life.

We have all seen those people who seem to lack skill but are able to pull off the most difficult tricks or have the ability to step well beyond their ability to attempt dangerous high-consequence tricks only to leave their friends watching with puzzled expressions on their face after they land it, while asking themselves how they were able to accomplish the trick so successfully. The short answer is that those athletes have a confidence and belief in themselves that they can and will land the trick. Since this high level of confidence is what we all want to adopt to allow for the greatest amount of progression let's first analyze the beliefs you should embrace to progress and those beliefs that are hindering your performance and should be dropped.

Positive and Negative Beliefs	
My sport is easy.	My sport is hard.
I learn (X) quickly.	I can't land new tricks.
I land my tricks all the time.	I learn (my sport) slowly.
I can learn any trick.	I'm going to hurt myself if I try new tricks.
I have the ability to be a great athlete.	I never land my tricks.
I have plenty of talent and skill.	I'm too fat/skinny /uncoordinated, to be a good athlete.
I am worthy.	
I am good enough.	I am worthless.
I am capable of doing anything I set my mind to.	I'm no good.
	I have no skill or talent.
I can achieve my goals.	I can't do anything.

Figure 11.
Uncovering your limiting beliefs is crucial for achieving your highest potential.

What Negative Beliefs do I Have Regarding my Sport/ Athletic Ability?

A great start is to simply ask yourself what negative beliefs you hold regarding your sport and ability and writing them down. Once you have uncovered as many as you can, ask yourself, "So what do I want?" The next step is to change all of the negative beliefs to their positive opposites, and write them down.

For example if you wrote down something like:

"I don't have enough skill to be a good athlete."

Then ask yourself "So what do I want?" Your answer might look like:

"I want to acquire the skill and talent necessary to be a great athlete. I will train daily, weekly, and monthly to improve my abilities."

This process changes your mindset, which will change your habits, which will change your results. Now take all of your limiting beliefs and ask yourself, "So what do I want," and write down your solutions, and scratch out the rest! Rewrite them all on a separate piece of paper and label it "Empowering Beliefs to Adopt."

What are Some Beliefs that Would Not Help me in my Sport?

Now ask yourself, "What are some beliefs that would not help me in my sport?" This time I want you to brainstorm all of the beliefs you could have that would prevent you from progressing in your athletic performance. Think of as many limiting beliefs as you can, and once you have written down every one that you can think of, ask yourself once again, "So what do I want?" Add all of the new answers to your list of Empowering Beliefs to Adopt.

What Beliefs Would a Pro Athlete Have Regarding Their Abilities?

What do you think a pro athlete believes about their abilities? What beliefs have they integrated completely? Think of as many empowering beliefs as you can as you imagine seeing the world through the eyes of some of the greatest athletes. You could use this same process to elicit empowering beliefs for any subject when you imagine the mind of someone who has already achieved greatness in their field. If you play basketball, for example, you can imagine Michael Jordan's mindset, or if you want to have success in business you can try and imagine what Richard Branson, Donald Trump, or Warren Buffet might believe about becoming a successful businessperson.

Now that you have taken the time to really dig deep and analyze your own limiting beliefs and elicited as many empowering beliefs as you can about your sport, make them into a list that you'll use in the next step. Figure 11 lists both positive and negative beliefs; however, make sure you *do your own* and add as many positive beliefs to it as possible!

THE BIG FIVE:
HOW YOU CAN PROGRAM YOUR MIND TO ACHIEVE ANYTHING YOU WANT THROUGH FIVE PROVEN PROCESSES

Research shows that it is completely possible to program our minds and create our realities through certain practices (Dispenza, 2014). These tools are used in psychology, advertising, therapy, and other fields every day. There are five proven processes that will help you to reprogram your belief system to an athletic mastery mindset. You will essentially be downloading your brain with new and better software. I encourage you to use these methods to analyze all aspects of your life and build a rock solid positive belief system for sport and, more importantly, for all aspects of who you are as a person.

Affirmations

Affirmations are short positive statements such as, "My sport is easy. I can land this trick. I will land this trick. I am a great athlete." Some people prefer to use short starter sentences to help them accept the affirmation more easily because if you say the words without believing them, then they will produce no effect in your mind. You must believe and internalize the affirmations you choose to use. Take, for example, the affirmation, "I am a great athlete." If you say these words and don't believe them to be true, the statement could cause a negative response. You can use the following starter phrases to help give your affirmations a better feeling.

- *"I love the thought of ...* landing this trick right now."
- *"I love the idea of ...* being a pro athlete."
- *"More and more ...* I am becoming a great (X)."
- *"I've decided ...* my sport is easy, and I will land my tricks every time."

Another affirmation trick is to add, "Why?" to your phrases. This will force you to come up with more solutions on how you can achieve your goals.

- *"Why am I a great athlete?* Because I train hard."
- *"Why do I grow more confident every day?* Because I visualize my tricks."
- *"Why am I now a sponsored athlete travelling the world?* Because I have worked hard and deserve it."

When you begin to use these affirmations throughout the days and weeks to come, you will begin the process of building new and more powerful core beliefs around your sport and athletic ability.

Positive Internal Dialogue (Self-Talk)

Positive self-talk is very similar to affirmations except this tactic is more focused on monitoring internal dialogue or what you tell yourself. This method requires you to be conscious of your thought processes and the things you tell yourself regarding sport and life. Whenever you catch yourself thinking something negative or self-defeating you need to stop that internal critic on the spot. If you hear yourself saying, "I suck at my sport," "I'm dumb," "I suck," "I can't do this," be sure to stop yourself mentally in that moment, and then ask yourself the very powerful and important question, "So what do I want?" and then focus your energy towards that positive and empowering answer.

- "I can't do (x) … So what do I want? I want to be able to do (x)."
- "I suck at sports … So what do I want? I love the thought of being a great athlete and learning quickly."
- "I'm dumb … So what do I want? I want to feel smarter and find my strengths."
- "I can't land this trick … So what do I want? I love the thought of being able to land this trick."
- "I'll never go pro … So what do I want? I love the thought of finding a way to make a life out of doing my sport."

It is critical you monitor your internal dialogue and change negative sentences to positive intentions at the very moment they occur. If you let yourself be carried away and don't stop the thought instantly it can lead to more and more negative thoughts, and you will strengthen your negative beliefs and internalize them even deeper.

Figure 12.
Recording your successes will help build your confidence.

Beyond sport it is important to be kind to yourself, most people in this world suffer needlessly because they torture themselves with negative self-talk. The bottom line is to attempt to rid your mind of all negative and limited internal dialogue. From this moment on whenever you catch yourself being critical or judgmental STOP and ask yourself, "So what do I want?" This simple and amazingly influential process will help you change the words, which will change your internal feeling, which will change your beliefs, which will change your results, which will inevitably change your life!

The Mental Trick Bag and Finding and Recording the Evidence

Finding and recording the evidence means celebrating your victories, even the small ones. If you notice yourself becoming more confident on a certain trick celebrate that; if you do something with more ease and style, record and recognize that; if you learn a new trick get excited and record that mentally or in your training log. You want to create what I call a "mental trick bag" of memories, which is a group of memories of you landing a specific trick. Once you build up about five memories of landing a specific trick you can go into your "mental trick bag" remember all the times you landed that trick and then go ahead and stomp it! The next part of this tactic is to be narrow minded, that is to say forget about the bad days, forget about the bails and how many times you had to fall to learn the trick, and focus on the one you landed! Your focus will dictate your future and the more you're able to focus on your progression the more you'll be hardwiring those beliefs into your mind, keep your focus on your successes both big and small.

Whenever you catch yourself thinking something negative or self-defeating, STOP and ask yourself: SO WHAT DO I WANT?

Swish Technique:

Imagine the feeling of going from scared to death to supremely confident, from feeling horrible to feeling ecstatic and turning any negative into a positive quickly and easily. Sounds good right? You're about to learn how you can do just that using the *swish technique*. This strategy comes from NLP and is both effortless and potent. Here's how it works. You must decide what you want to change, find the triggers, create the positive imagery of what you want, and swish or in common language, switch the images from what you *don't* want to what you *do* want. The first thing you need to do is get clear on what thought, feeling, belief, or habit you want to change. You can achieve this by asking yourself, "So what do I want?" If you're not confident then you want to feel confident. If you don't want to fall, then you want to land the trick. Make sure you are clear on the positive outcome you are trying to achieve.

The second step is to figure out what causes or sets off these thoughts; in NLP terms, you must identify the trigger. If competition day causes fear and lack of confidence start there, or maybe it should be when you're getting to the place where you practice. If you want to increase your confidence, but every time you see certain people or go certain places it causes uneasiness and a lack of confidence, all of those are triggers too. It's best to identify where and what your triggers are so that when you are faced with the circumstances you are ready with a solution. These unwanted feelings can also happen randomly at which point you can use the swish pattern on the spot; however, there are usually certain places, people, or experiences that trigger these feelings naturally and continuously.

Now it's time to create a mental image of what you want to happen. You can create an image or you can use a memory of a time when you had the feeling you're trying to recreate. If you want more confidence you can build an image in your mind of how you look and feel when you are extremely confident, or you can remember a time in your life when you felt extreme confidence and use that memory. The important idea is to use an image that brings up the most powerful feelings of what you desire to achieve. Continue to enhance the detail and quality of your mental image so that it's crystal clear and powerful.

Now you are ready to apply the swish pattern. Using your mind's eye first imagine you are sitting in a movie theatre with a massive screen directly in front of you. First you will project the image of the unwanted feeling, belief, or habit you want to change. View the image from your seat in the theatre from a dissociated perspective, and then in the top left corner of your mental screen place the positive solution image you've created.

The next step is to slowly switch or "swish" the two images. As you look at the screen in your mind's eye begin switching the images and making the image in the top left hand corner bigger and bigger while making the unwanted image go smaller and farther away. As your new wanted image comes onto the screen make it big, bright, and clear, and this time associate with the positive image and feel all the feelings of confidence or feelings that you desire as the unwanted image fades and disappears into the background.

Continue to repeat this process a minimum of ten times or until you feel your body and mind integrate the positive feeling completely. Each time you go through the process be sure to clear your mind even if only for a second, and then do it again. Gradually swish the images slowly at first (take about ten seconds), and gradually increase the swish speed so that by the last round you are switching them almost instantly.

Another example of how you might use this pattern is if you were looking for more confidence. You would have the image of you acting nervous or insecure on the big screen and the mental image of confidence you desire in the top left corner waiting to be swished in. You can use a past experience when you were extremely confident or simply create a very strong feeling of confidence in your mind's eye by imagining what confidence feels like in great detail. As long as you have an emotion, thought, or feeling that won't go away you can always use the swish technique to bring you back to the positive.

Fake It Until You Make It

I'm sure you've heard the expression, "Fake it until you make it." The concept of faking it until you make it doesn't mean being a fraud or pretending that you're something you're not. The power and effectiveness of this technique comes from the process of visualization, positive thinking, and belief programming, which ultimately changes your way of thinking and your habits, beliefs, and outcomes.

When you fake it or pretend that you've already achieved your goal, whether that is to be a pro athlete, own your own business, or have the girl of your dreams, you spend a good amount of time hardwiring your brain to achieve those things, you show your brain that not only it's possible but you *expect* it to happen and there is tremendous power in expectation.

All you need to do is to spend time day dreaming about what it will feel like when you're a pro athlete or have that beautiful girlfriend at your side. How will you carry yourself? How will you feel? What will it be like? As you imagine all of this, your subconscious mind, the universe, laws of attraction, or whatever you'd like to call it works to make that feeling and image a reality.

Many people stay stuck where they are because they don't believe they can achieve their goals. The truth is that we are all infinitely powerful and capable of anything. When you wake up every day feeling excited and go throughout your day imagining that you've achieved your goal, your mind will work ferociously to make it happen. You'll begin to attract the correct training, people, resources, circumstances, and create the deep internal motivation to make it a reality. To accomplish anything you have to first have a vision, then you need to believe in yourself and the possibility of making that happen, and finally move towards the feeling of what it's going to be like when you've achieved it.

This process is not something new and the fact is that it's been passed down from generation to generation by some of the greatest minds in history. Now you can use this advice and get very clear on what your vision is, then live like it's already here, and finally get the feeling of what reaching your goal is like.

THE SIMPLE AND SAFE WAY TO MAKE POWERFUL SELF-HYPNOSIS RECORDINGS THAT WILL FORCE YOUR MIND TO ACCOMPLISH WHATEVER YOU ASK

Undoubtedly self-hypnosis is one of the most powerful processes you can use to achieve your goals because it fuses visualization, affirmation, and positive reinforcement of your goals all in one technique. The sad part is that the stigma surrounding hypnosis is mostly negative; however, most people are still intrigued by its mystery.

First and foremost realize hypnosis is simple, powerful, and extremely effective! Forget everything you've ever heard about hypnosis. The perception of hypnosis has become incredibly skewed and is seen as hokey when the fact is that self-hypnosis, clinical hypnosis, and sports hypnosis have been used for years to help top athletes achieve their goals. It is essentially a combination of meditation and positive self-talk. Self-hypnosis works in the same way as your guided visualization process except it will include more suggestions, affirmations, and positive self-talk that you create. In the simplest terms you enter into a relaxed state where your mind is more open, you have more access to your unconsciousness where your core beliefs are stored and your ability to receive and internalize new suggestions increases dramatically. Since you are in a relaxed state you don't have your conscious mind or, in hypnosis terms, critical factor interrupting every second with its limiting beliefs, doubt, and distraction.

Hypnosis works by bypassing your critical factor or conscious mind and implanting positive suggestions and visualizations that will lead you closer to your goals. The Russian Olympic team took 11 hypnotists to the 1956 Melbourne Olympics to help the athletes with visualization and to develop mental clarity. The Russians won more medals that year than any other country (Cunningham, 1984). Within the community of top athletes some form of sports hypnosis is not only recommended it is essentially mandatory. When you learn the process of self-hypnosis, you don't have to pay hundreds or thousands of dollars to hire a sports psychologist or sports hypnotist to get incredible results. The process is extremely simple. It is unnecessary to read a bunch of books or take courses on hypnosis to reap the benefits; you simply have to follow this bare bones process.

Imagine ten minutes from now being able to make simple and easy recordings that will hardwire your mind to manifest and create exactly what you narrate. As you think about all the ways you can use self-hypnosis—from helping you become a phenomenal athlete to increasing concentration to achieving more success to overcoming fear—you might start to get excited because you can use it to help you with anything you desire. Muhammad Ali put it best when he said, "It's the repetition of affirmations that lead to belief. And once that belief becomes a deep conviction things begin to happen."

Self-hypnosis is similar to a guided visualization except you'll be using more direct commands for your *unconscious mind to obey*. All you need is a recording device to get started; there are many options such as your phone or computer. You don't need anything special or extravagant, anything that will record your voice will work.

Read an Induction or Relaxation Script

The purpose of an induction or relaxation script is to put you in a relaxed state of mind; there are many different types of relaxation scripts to choose from; however, it's important to put yourself into a state of relaxation and use your induction script to deepen your relaxation. Meditation is an excellent practice. You can use any option from the guided visualization component because the goal is the same: to get you clear-minded and relaxed. The countdown from ten to one method is very effective as is the quick relaxation script, or anything else that you create. The complete Zen Athlete online program has several different relaxation audios you can choose from. The process of self-hypnosis is exactly like a guided visualization except this time you're going to focus more on suggestions and modifications to your core beliefs. The induction part is simply an aid to help you clear your mind and get into a relaxed, receptive state where you can visualize and focus clearly so choose whatever method you prefer and feel free to experiment. Here is a brief example of an induction script so you get the idea.

Begin by closing your eyes and taking a deep breath in through your nose and relax as much as possible. Now as you continue to breathe and continue to relax bring your attention to your feet. Now that you are completely focused on your feet you can allow them to relax completely. Now slowly and gently move your awareness up to your legs and allow them to relax as deeply as possible. As you allow yourself to relax deeper and deeper you notice your legs and feet are completely relaxed. Now as your body continues to relax move your awareness up to your hips and your stomach and allow a warm soothing energy to completely relax your abdomen, hips and lower body ....

Our deepest fear is not that we are inadequate. Our deepest fear is that we are powerful beyond measure.

— Marianne Williamson

Create Your Personalized Mental Programmer Script

Here is the part where you get to have some fun and decide what exactly you want to accomplish. This is where you design your script in detail, describing all of your goals and hardwiring your brain to bring them into reality. In this section you can use your ideal beliefs, affirmations, or mental commands.

- "You have the discipline to train daily."
- "You will now perform your sport four or more times every week."
- "You have fantastic flexibility from stretching every day."
- "You learn tricks faster because you visualize your tricks daily."

Mix commands and affirmations with descriptive detailed visualizations and you will have yourself a personalized script. Here are a few examples from the list we created earlier.

- "You have the ability to land any trick you set your mind to. Imagine yourself easily landing all of the tricks you're trying to learn."
- "Your sport comes easily and naturally to you."
- "You learn tricks quickly and constantly progress your ability. See yourself six months from now confidently doing all the tricks you want. Feel the confidence and what it's like to land all of the tricks easily."
- "You can now easily land a backside 360 (or any other specific trick). Visualize yourself now going off the jump and spinning a back 3 effortlessly. Watch yourself spin smoothly and confidently knowing you're going to land it perfectly."

Simply write down your clear affirmations and give yourself commands and describe your goals in detail; it's that simple! You'll now record your written script consisting of your affirmations, goals, and beliefs you want to adopt. Be sure to describe them clearly and in as much detail as you'd can. You can speak slowly and have fun visualizing yourself having and experiencing all of the things you're trying to manifest. Here's another example to show you how easy it is.

> You are in the process of becoming an amazing athlete, see yourself learning more and more tricks. You are progressing your skills naturally and easily. See yourself land all the tricks you want to learn. You learn quickly. You land your tricks every time. More and more you are becoming an incredible athlete. See yourself two months from now landing all of the tricks you are trying to learn right now.

The more vivid a picture you can paint in your mind, the more effect it will have. Make it a spectacular, big, and bright movie that you'll love watching in your mind's eye. The best way to get started is to record a couple of different scripts you have written. After you listen to one or two of your recordings you'll feel more comfortable with the process, and you'll be able to fine-tune your scripts. You'll get better at describing what you want to accomplish, and you'll come up with more beliefs and suggestions that you want to adopt. I recommend you begin your recording with the suggestion, "My mind and body are going to accept all of these suggestions," or something similar because it is a powerful intention to begin your sessions with.

Return to Full Awareness

Contrary to what some people believe you are not a zombie when under hypnosis, especially when you perform it yourself; you're simply in a meditative state. When you are ready to finish the recording begin to countdown from five to one, suggesting with each count that you are becoming more and more awake, and end with, "At the count of one, you open your eyes feeling fully refreshed." If you wish to continue relaxing and visualizing your tricks or goals in this powerful state of mind, you can choose to ignore the suggestion to come back to full awareness and continue for as long as you desire. It is a good idea to end your session with a positive intention.

- "You have accepted all of these suggestions, and you are on your way to achieving all of your goals."
- "You are going to awaken full of vibrant energy, fully revitalized, and ready to have a great day."
- "You are going to open your eyes with a burst of energy and excitement for your day knowing you're well on your way to achieving your goals."

Mental Training Tip

If you have any recording software like Garage Band you can add relaxing background music to help with your relaxation and focus.

Self-hypnosis is simple, straightforward, and very effective. When you make and listen to your first recording you'll immediately understand why. Remember there is no exact script you have to follow to make it work. All you need to do is relax yourself, read a script with positive suggestions, and have your mind visualize and experience those suggestions. As you're in this powerful, relaxed, and receptive state your mind will begin building new neural pathways and essentially start programming what you visualize to become reality. When you follow the outline, keep hypnosis simple, and begin experimenting with the technique you'll quickly get tremendous results. This is one of the most powerful and potent tools anyone can use for sport, business, and life to achieve more success. This is the golden ticket for shaping your mind and creating your reality, and if you who decide to follow through and experiment, you'll have the joy of realizing the immense power of self-hypnosis and use it in all aspects of your life.

Belief in yourself and your abilities is all you need to succeed. These strategies are designed to help you reveal your current limiting beliefs, uncover the most beneficial beliefs to adopt, and, finally, internalize them so that you have the best chance at success. All of the techniques are scientifically tested and proven. I wonder if you're imagining all the different ways you can shape and design your life by using them.

Complete This Challenge

It's time to put all these strategies to good use. Your challenge for the confidence component is intended to ensure you will be able to apply and experience the techniques of self-hypnosis. Record two very brief (five to ten minutes) self-hypnosis audios.

First come up with a list of your possible negative beliefs. Once you have that list ask yourself, "So what do I want?" and come up with a list of beliefs you would prefer to have. Once you have the positive list turn each belief into an affirmation. Once you have done all of that it will be easy to experiment with the swish technique. The goal is to ensure you experiment with the strategies because when you follow the steps outlined here you'll realize how easy and powerful they truly are. See Figure 11 for examples.

GOAL SETTING

DEDICATION

FITNESS & NUTRITION

SIMULATION

ZEN

FOCUS

BELIEF

MEDITATION

VISUALIZATION

SIMULATION

Let's take flight simulation as an example. If you're trying to train a pilot, you can simulate almost the whole course. You don't have to get in an airplane until late in the process.
—Roy Romer

MASTERING YOUR MOVEMENTS

The application of simulation training is the magic formula for progressing your performance beyond what you think possible. Experts in many areas other than sports such as technology, education, and space exploration use simulation to help further their knowledge and results. Astronauts will simulate various scenarios hundreds even thousands of times until they have all but mastered it because they could be faced with a life or death situation. In your case, your success or failure will only affect you. The more you apply simulation training the less you will fall and the faster you'll learn the movements, skills or tricks.

Simulation is simply trying to simulate the trick or maneuver you're trying to learn as closely as possible. You can apply specific simulation training and do drills that focus on one trick and you can also apply general simulation training by taking part in games, sports, or activities that are similar to your sport. A few great examples of general simulation training are yoga, trampoline, or skateboarding. The key to making simulation training as effective as possible is to make the simulation as real as possible and focus on technique, balance, and the feeling of the simulation. In what ways can you think of applying simulation training to your sport? If you're a skateboarder, snowboarder, or skier you can use balance boards or model the moves at home or on the trampoline just to name a few. If you're into mountain biking, skydiving, or racing you may have to come up with some creative solutions to model the movements you'll be doing.

SIX CROSS TRAINING SPORTS TO ELEVATE YOUR PERFORMANCE

Simulation training can be very specific to a move or it can be more general where you develop skills that can transfer to your sport. Cross training in multiple disciplines will help you add new types of skills, balance, and strength to your repertoire as well as keep your training fresh. Any sport or activity that keeps you in shape, helps build muscle, balance, endurance, or coordination can be considered general simulation training. Here are six fantastic sports you can use to supplement your training to build skill in your discipline.

Yoga

Yoga is one of the best and most effective cross training or simulation activities you can do to improve your balance and mobility. Yoga builds strength, balance, and flexibility. It also teaches you concentration, awareness, and breath work, which will come in handy as you get better and push yourself farther. Yoga is heavily rooted in mental and spiritual practices and will help you not only improve physically but also mentally. You can expect to improve your concentration, awareness, and meditation practice. You'll also learn how to control and understand your states of mind better, and your overall mental game will improve immensely.

Gymnastics

If you've ever seen any Olympic Games or even a mediocre gymnast in action then you realize how training in gymnastics would be beneficial to your athletic performance. Gymnasts are incredibly strong, flexible, and have mind-blowing air awareness. Practicing gymnastics doesn't mean simply putting on some spandex and walking the balance beam. There are many aspects you can learn. Many gymnastics studios offer open gym times, meaning you can go in there and jump, flip, spin, and land on padded mats so you can simulate all the tricks you're trying to learn without risking your biscuits on the snow!

Figure 13.
Matthew Belair having some fun surfing and jumping around in Nicaragua.

Free Running/Parkour

Free running or parkour has exploded onto the scene in the last five years, and its popularity continues to grow. Parkour is a discipline based on body movement aiming to get you from point A to point B as efficiently as possible. It has evolved into an urban acrobatic sport with athletes pushing the boundaries daily by doing bigger flips, jumping bigger gaps, and taking bigger risks in their urban playgrounds.

Surfing

Probably the purest board sport of them all. Surfing requires a combination of strength, stamina, balance, and most of all persistence and strong will because the learning curve is difficult but the rewards are worth it. The feeling of turning on fresh powder and the feeling of catching a beautiful wave are both indescribable and addictive. Many athletes change sports in the off season to keep active, learn new skills, and enjoy something new.

Martial Arts

Most disciplines of martial arts focus on three different and equally important elements of development, which are mind, body, and spirit. Extreme sports and martial arts are mirrors of each other in many ways and complement each other wonderfully. Both focus on self-development and expression. No matter what discipline of martial arts you decide to practice, whether it's MMA, boxing, Kung Fu, Tai Chi, you'll be guaranteed to learn many applicable lessons to improve the performance in your sport.

Figure 14.
Surfing requires a combination of strength, stamina, balance, and, most of all, persistence and strong will.

Slacklining

Slacklining is essentially tight rope walking except the rope's tension is adjusted to create different levels of difficulty. Slacklining will develop your balance and it's a fun way to pass the time at the beach or in the park. Once you've mastered simply walking the line, which in itself is no easy task, you can continue to up your progression with a variety of tricks and maneuvers.

Figure 14 and 15.
The photo on the left is Matthew Belair and his Sifu, a 34th degree Shaolin kung fu master. They are at a temple in China where they trained. The photo on the right was taken in a gym in Thailand where Belair trained MMA for six weeks. Both experiences were very difficult and rewarding.

The application of
simulation training is
the magic formula for
progressing your athletic
ability beyond what you
think possible, faster than
you think possible.

THE HIDDEN POWER OF WATCHING VIDEOS

Most athletes are able to watch videos of their sport religiously and are unaware of the hidden power and influence it has on their performance. Watching video clips is always fun because athletes are creative, talented, and can do mind-blowing tricks. As we watch the video clips we get excited because we imagine ourselves being in those places and performing the tricks unconsciously and sometimes even consciously. The old expression "monkey see, monkey do" comes to mind to help explain the incredible power watching videos has on you and how we can amplify its effect easily.

Each time you see an athlete perform a trick you're unconsciously learning and teaching yourself without even knowing it. If you're watching a video on YouTube and you're a man watching another man get kicked in the nuts, it almost hurts doesn't it? The same is true for most painful fail videos we watch because it's almost impossible for us not to put ourselves in the athletes' shoes. The exact same processes are happening to you as you watch videos of your sport, which causes you to slowly program yourself to achieve what you see. With each viewing and repetition your mind and body are growing more and more familiar with the techniques. Now that you're mindful of the power of watching video parts I'm going to teach you a sneaky tactic that will turn watching videos into a dangerously effective training process.

The next time you throw on a vid and watch it with your buddies or watch an athlete on YouTube you're going to practice something called *active viewing*. As you watch the video rather than just sitting back you're going to actively focus on pretending that you're the athlete performing the technique. Really try and get into the feeling of doing each and every movement. This will work just like an active guided visualization and have a similarly powerful effect. The other strategy that you can experiment with when active viewing is to pretend you're actually the athlete and you're watching and pretending to be them. When the athlete you're watching comes onto the screen I want you to imagine that you are the athlete and completely step into the role. This method really helps you build your confidence and sense of the trick because if you're pretending to be them you're going to adopt some of their beliefs and you can just enjoy pretending to do all of the tricks without your limiting beliefs about your skill level getting in the way.

Simulation training is simple and fantastically effective. When you use these guidelines to begin training and come up with specific simulation drills for what you're trying to learn you'll be shocked with the results after a few short weeks. Make simulation training your own practice and come up with new and creative ways to model the maneuvers. Any training that you do to specifically model a technique will help tremendously.

BECOME THE BEST BY SURROUNDING YOURSELF WITH THE BEST

Many great thinkers have suggested that having a great mentor or coach is the fastest way to develop your skills and talents. I have always utilized the strategy of learning from the best in the world to develop my skills. When I wanted to improve my snowboarding, I moved to Whistler, British Columbia, Canada, and rode more than 100 days a year with some of the best snowboarders on the planet. When I wanted to master my mind and learn about meditation, I spent five weeks in Nepal with Buddhist monks living, eating, and breathing their way of life. When I wanted to learn about the law of attraction, how to be a great coach and speaker, I mentored under the world renowned author of *Law of Attraction*, Michael J. Losier. When I wanted to become a better martial artist, I trained at Phuket Top Team, a world class mixed martial arts gym in Thailand with professionals. Finally, when I wanted to discover what I was capable of and learn from real super humans, I visited a 34th Generation Shaolin temple in China and trained with Kung Fu Masters who could smash granite with all of their limbs including just two fingers!

Intuitively this just made sense to me. If I wanted to be the best at something, I would have to surround myself with and learn from the best. Now we have the science that backs this theory up in the form of mirror neurons. Mirror neurons are neurons in the brain that react to our observation of the environment. As we observe our environment, research has shown that mirror neurons will fire in the same way through observation and when we perform the operation ourselves (Dispenza, 2014). We are essentially programming the skills through observation!

Surrounding yourself with the best just makes sense. You will eat, sleep, and breathe the pinnacle of your sport. You will observe peoples' habits, training routines, and beliefs, and discover a way of thinking and a way of life. You'll unconsciously and consciously absorb a new way of thinking.

There is also the likelihood of having the best terrain and resources necessary to elevate your game. It is difficult to become the best big mountain skier in the world if you train at a small resort. Your environment and surroundings shape who you are in every way. Choose an environment that will cultivate the skills that you want to develop.

Complete This Challenge

To get you into the swing of things, your challenge for the simulation component is to come up with three simulation exercises you can do to help you learn the trick you're trying to learn. If you're a skateboarder that might mean taking your board on the trampoline, a snowboarder might practice jumping at home, a biker might practice simple spins on the grass. Come up with three creative ways to learn a trick or maneuver you're trying to learn, and add it to your training.

GOAL SETTING

DEDICATION

FITNESS & NUTRITION

ZEN

FOCUS

SIMULATION

BELIEF

MEDITATION

VISUALIZATION

NUTRITION AND FITNESS

If a man achieves victory over this body, who in the world can exercise power over him? He who rules himself rules over the whole world.
—*Vinoba Bhave*

ESSENTIAL NUTRITION AND FITNESS KNOWLEDGE

A few months from now you may look back at this second as a critical moment in your life. The world of food is confusing and unfortunately extremely horrific and mind blowing once you begin looking into things. This component will give you a crash course in food and diet that will hopefully change your perspective forever. The reality is that most extreme sports athletes don't consider any type of fitness or nutrition education and implementation, which is precisely why you're about to be leagues ahead of everyone else. After years of research into fitness and nutrition I have finally discovered what works best and what doesn't.

The first thing we are going to cover is nutrition and food. There is tremendous power in food and diet to the point that it affects our brain chemistry. Just a little research into what goes into food, how meat is processed, or even looking at the ingredients of what you're eating may shock you; everyday food is literally killing you, and I'm not being melodramatic. If you're young and active you may not notice it much, but when you begin to eat cleaner and healthier you'll notice your energy levels skyrocket. Keep in mind this book is designed for elite athletes and if you're looking to achieve your full potential you must be aware of what you're eating. Food is what the body needs to grow, provides you energy, and sustains life. If you consistently eat garbage your body won't be able to give you the high returns you need to develop all of the muscles and stamina you need. Here are a few tips you can apply today to get you on the right track.

SIMPLE TIPS TO EATING HEALTHIER AND UNDERSTANDING FOOD

The Power of the Food Pyramid: The Ultimate Cheat Sheet

Simply be conscious of what you are putting into your body. When you eat, pay attention to how you feel afterwards because some foods give you energy and others can make you feel like you need a nap. When you keep the food pyramid in mind and attempt to make a conscious effort of eating enough fruits, vegetables, and healthy foods per day, you're already on your way to improving your diet and energy levels.

Do Not Skip Breakfast

I'm sure you've heard this one before, and it's because it's important! Even if you can manage something quick it's important since research shows people who do not eat breakfast are heavier because eating in the morning gets your metabolism up and running for the rest of the day. If you skip breakfast, you skip revving your metabolism.

Eat Less Fast Food and Junk

If you're regularly eating at McDonalds, drinking liters of soda, and pounds of chips and candy then it's time to monitor your eating habits. It's certainly fine to eat junk food but keeping everything in moderation will not only help your body, but if you don't you could end up with some seriously negative side effects when you get older. At the same time if you want to become an elite athlete you have to eat right. Professional sports teams don't have their pre- or post-game meals at Burger King.

Eat Smaller Meals

Overeating and stuffing yourself is another common problem. Fit in light meals when you can and you will avoid overeating. Remember it takes time for your body to process and realize it's full. Also having healthy snacks prevents you from stuffing yourself and feeling bloated and lazy.

Eat Slowly

Eating slowly has two major benefits. The first is that eating slower will allow your brain and stomach some time to communicate and realize you are full, which means you will be less likely to overeat. The other benefit is that the more you chew the more you get to know the real power of food the more it will shock you. There are many examples of people who were diagnosed with terminal illnesses who completely changed their diets to eat natural, whole foods, and healed themselves. Most holistic doctors will first ask you about your diet before providing any diagnosis, what you eat will either heal you and give you energy or suck the life out of you and cause disease. The best idea is to start right now and little by little continue to educate yourself on healthy eating habits because it might be the most important thing you can do for yourself.

THE FOODS THAT ARE ZAPPING YOUR ENERGY, CREATING DISEASE, AND SLOWLY KILLING YOU

The chances are high that you probably know someone who's a vegetarian, gluten free, or declares themselves a conscious eater of one sort or another. I'm sure you can also think of someone who is suffering physically and possibly was even hospitalized due to a lifetime of poor eating habits. There is a massive consciousness shift regarding food because the statistics are staggering. If you've seen any food documentaries such as *Food, Inc.* or you've looked into what you're eating in the slightest then you are aware of the madness that is the food industry.

If you think it's is a little over dramatic to say food can zap your energy and is slowly kill you, here are some sobering facts from the Institute of Health Metrics and Evaluation at the University of Washington (2010). A 2010 study showed the top ten risk factors for health loss and the number of deaths attributed to each one. Diet and poor nutrition topped the list ahead of smoking at a whopping 678,282 people in the US alone! I know you might be thinking that you're young and healthy and this doesn't apply to you, but you couldn't be more wrong. Even if you feel great, when you discover that most easy, accessible, and normal everyday food has detrimental effects on the body and in a few short years could cause serious illness, you'll want to change the way you eat, never mind trying to become a serious athlete on a poor diet. Treat food as fuel for the body. Imagine eating at an all you can eat KFC buffet before running a marathon.

You would be sluggish and have a hard time meeting your time goal. The meals you eat have a similar but lesser effect on your daily energy levels and performance.

The sole purpose of this component is to encourage you to begin to look at food in an entirely new light. Imagine yourself six months from now having twice as much energy, feeling lighter and stronger, and with a deep sense of personal satisfaction because you now understand the difference between using healthy food instead of poison to fuel your body. Figure 19 lists some of the worst foods to avoid and ideas for healthy alternatives. I'm not suggesting you have to cut the bad foods out completely, although that would be ideal, but be conscious of how often you eat them and focus on choosing healthy alternatives.

When interviewing food expert Adam Hart, the author of the Power of Food, on my podcast he recommended we eat whole foods, make our own sauces, and add seeds, such as hemp and chia seeds wherever we can. Some good alternatives you can use from the list in Figure 19 are natural honey as sweetener, water or natural juices or green tea for beverages, avocadoes and quinoa for meat. As you begin to learn more and more about food you'll realize there is a healthy alternative to everything. Although it does take some getting used to, once your body experiences proper nutrition it will never want to go back.

A superfood is anything that is high in nutritional value. It contains more of the necessary nutrients that give the body energy. Eating superfoods can be compared to fueling up a dragster with high octane fuel. Regular fuel might cut it but you certainly won't get the same performance.

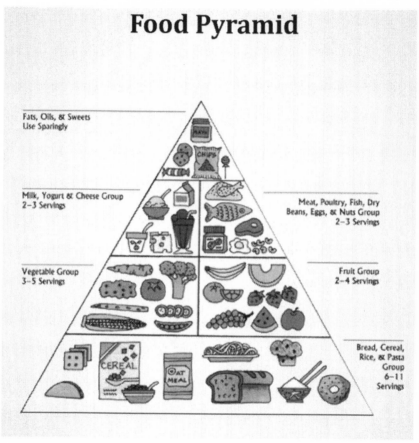

Figure 17.
The food pyramid is a good guide for healthy food choices.

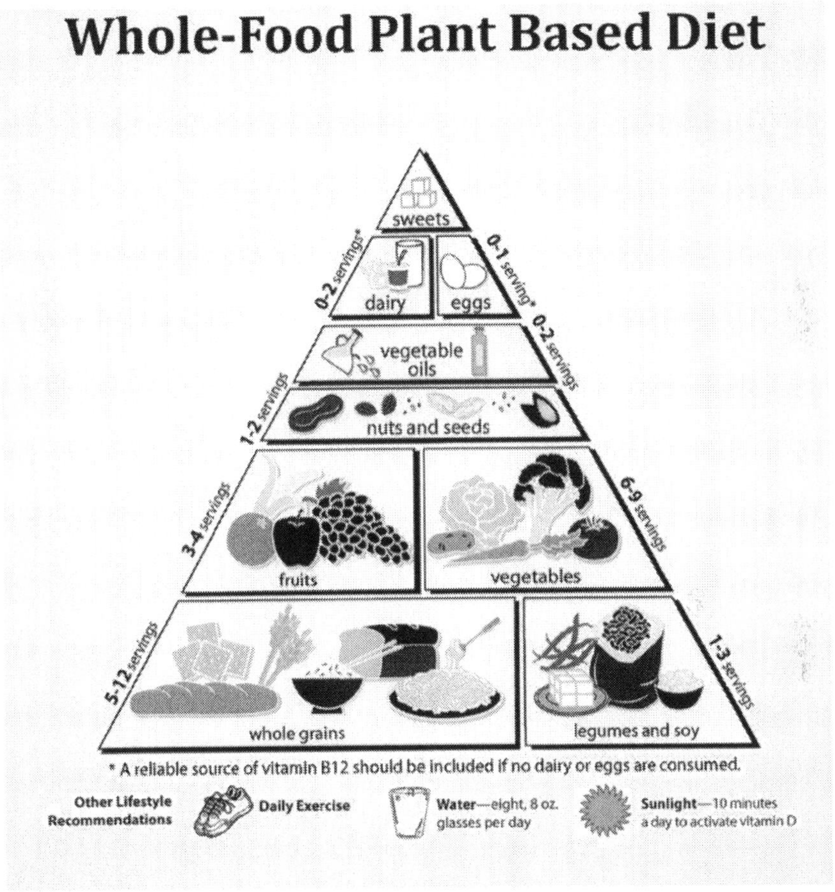

Whole-Food Plant Based Diet

Figure 18.
Those on a plant based diet also have a
food pyramid to use as a guide to healthy eating.

The food you eat can be either the safest and most powerful form of medicine or the slowest form of poison.

—Ann Wigmore
—Jiddu Krishnamurti

This chapter is a quick and dirty overview of all you need to get on the right track to healthy eating, and you should now realize how harmful food can be when misused, and how powerful food can be when eaten properly. If you're interested in looking into the subject a little more the Internet is overflowing with information on how to get the most out of food so you can take advantage of that at any time and increase your knowledge. You'll be eating for the rest of your life so learning how to cook and what food does to your body is invaluable.

The doctor of the future will no longer treat the human frame with drugs but will rather cure and prevent disease with nutrition.

—Thomas Edison

Foods to Avoid	Healthy Alternatives
All energy drinks	Water, coconut water, green tea
Soda pop	Water, water with lemon or lime, natural juice
Processed foods	Whole foods, fruit, nuts
Fast food	Whole foods
Chips	Apple, banana, other fruit.
Processed meat	Free range unprocessed meat, avocado, vegetables
	Honey
Processed sugar	Make your own
Sauces like ketchup, BBQ sauces, mayo, dressing	
Fried foods	A grilled or baked version
Donuts	Healthy snack
Ice cream	Healthy snack
Dairy	Healthy snack
Margarine	Butter
Artificial sweeteners	Honey

Figure 19.
Be conscious of how often you eat unhealthy food and make an effort to choose healthier options.

Bonus List of 53 Super Foods

Avocados	Cantaloupe	Oranges
Kale	Carrots	Papaya
Coconut and coconut oil	Cauliflower	Peaches
	Cherries	Pineapple
Quinoa	Chia seeds	Pumpkin
Almonds	Dark chocolate	Pomegranates
Apples	Eggs	Spirulina
Apricots	Fish	Spinach
Artichokes	Flax seeds	Tomatoes
Asparagus	Garlic	Swiss chard
Bananas	Hot peppers	Sweet potatoes
Beans and lentils	Grapes	Walnuts
Beets	Kiwi	Almonds
Bell peppers	Lemons	Goji berries
Berries	Limes	Hemp seeds
Broccoli	Mangoes	Bok choy
Cabbage	Low fat yogurt and cottage cheese	Mushrooms
Oats		Ginger
Olive oil		

Figure 20.
Superfoods give your body the energy it needs to perform its best.

LITTLE KNOWN SECRETS TO ACHIEVING OLYMPIC FITNESS LEVELS

Now that you understand the basics of nutrition you are in for a treat. By the end of this component, not only will you have the most effective workouts and strategies to keep fit but I will reveal to you a training strategy that has the potential to double your athletic skill. Before we get there, however, let's first analyze physical attributes that would be ideal for athletes.

- **Strong Core**: Aids in balance and generates power for spins.
- **Flexible**: Makes it easier for your body to perform tricks and leads to less injuries.
- **Minimal Body fat**: Makes it easier to perform tricks.
- **Strong legs**: Help with pop, balance, control, and endurance.
- **Good balance**: Essential for all sports.
- **High endurance**: Makes it easier to practice longer before tiring, reducing injuries caused by fatigue.

Now that we know what body type and physical attributes will help us become better athletes let's look at some ways we can begin developing these attributes.

Seven Fun Ways to Get Into Phenomenal Shape

Play a Sport. With so many sports to choose from pick any one of them to be involved in since any sport will demand you stay in shape and playing sports is always fun.

Skateboarding. Skateboarding is a tremendously difficult sport that is fun and forces you to master many useful athletic skills such as balance, timing, strength, and persistence.

Free Running. Free running, a new sport that's exploded in popularity in recent years, is a good option since you can add some free running to your jogs to make it more exciting.

Martial Arts. There are many different kinds of martial arts available to learn, all of which teach you how to develop your mind and body. After doing some research on the many styles of martial arts most people find one they really enjoy.

Surfing. Surfing is certainly one of the most difficult activities anyone can choose but with time and dedication you'll soon get the hang of it. Surfing requires strength, cardio, balance, and mental toughness. If you ever get the chance, get a board and jump into the water.

Yoga. Yoga is a practice that strengthens and stretches the body. It is a very similar practice to martial arts where it goes beyond the physical into the mental and spiritual realms. Developing a consistent yoga practice is a surefire way to improve your game.

Gymnastics. There is no shortage of technique, flexibility, and strength in gymnastics. If you are looking for a new way to challenge yourself this would be the way to do it.

Any of these fun options will help you get into great shape in a fun and exciting way. Adding some specific exercises will help you develop all the strength and muscles you need to achieve your highest potential. All you need to do is pick a few exercises and decide the number of repetitions or time and sets.

THE TEN CRITICAL STRETCHES FOR DEVELOPING DYNAMIC MOBILITY

You're about to discover a little known and critical part of athletic training: being flexible in the right places helps your performance in countless ways.

Stretch daily and get in the habit of stretching throughout the day; stretch while watching TV, while watching online videos, during downtime, and whenever you can. It's better to stretch for short periods multiple times throughout the day than during one big session. Stretching can be a little boring that's why doing it when you are distracted will help you stretch more consistently.

Remember when stretching to only do what feels right and exercise caution. Stretching is not supposed to hurt; it can be uncomfortable but should not hurt. You can stretch for periods of time for example 10, 20, or up to 60 seconds at a time and repeat the stretch ensuring you're only doing what *feels* right.

1. **Deep Squat hip stretch**: Start from standing and drop down into as low of a squat as you can go and feel your hips and groin stretch.

2. **Head to Knee:** Either standing or sitting keep your legs straight and reach your hands forward to touch your toes, stretching your hamstrings.

3. **Butterfly Stretch**: Start sitting with legs out in front of you. Now pull your feet in with the bottoms of your feet facing each other. Keep your back as straight as you can and use your elbows to push your knees down or lean forward to stretch the groin.

4. **Standing Quad Stretch**: Start from a standing position and bring one foot up behind you and grab it. Pull your heel towards your buttock to stretch your quad. Repeat with the other leg.

5. **Lunge**: Step one foot forward and keep your other leg behind you. Your front foot should be under your knee and you should feel the stretch in your hip flexor. You can also drop your knee and push the stretch as far as comfortable. Repeat with the other leg.

6. **Seated Twist**: Begin with both feet out in front of you sitting on the ground. Bring one foot close to your body and cross it over your leg while leaving the other leg extended. Extend your spine towards the sky and begin rotating in the opposite direction using your knee to add resistance. Repeat with the other leg.

7. **Static Figure Four**: Start by lying on your back, pull your right knee halfway to your chest and place your left ankle over your right knee then add resistance by pulling up your right side. Repeat for left side.

8. **Lying Leg Pull Over**: Start by lying flat on your back, bring one knee up into your chest and then pull it across your body slowly then turn your head in the opposite direction stretching your glutes and spine. Repeat with the other side.

9. **Lying Quad Stretch**: Lie down on your side and bring one foot back and grab it with the corresponding hand. Add resistance by pulling your foot towards your buttocks and stretching your quad as much as you can. Repeat on the other side.

10. **Pigeon Pose**: Begin on all fours. Bring your right knee forward towards your right wrist. Then, place your ankle near your left hip at approximately a 45-degree angle. Slide your left leg back while straightening your knee and pointing your toe. Begin to lower yourself down keeping your hips square. Repeat on the other side.

A SIMPLE AND EFFECTIVE GUIDE TO BUILDING SUPERHUMAN STRENGTH AND POWER

There is a world of information out there on how to build strength. Pavel Tsatsouline is widely recognized as one of the best coaches in the world for increasing pure strength. He has spent a lifetime dissecting the best routines and goes completely against convention with a minimalist approach. Using his methods, I went from deadlifting 215 pounds to 415 pounds in just over three months! Here are two training programs he recommends for building superhuman strength.

Routine #1: Choose three to five exercises, and do one set of five repetitions. Yes, only one set of five! Choose between deadlift, squat, overhead press, weighted chin-up, and weighted dip. Complete the workout five days on and one day off. The routine works because of consistency and not by overloading and exhausting the muscles (Tsatsouline, 2000).

Routine # 2: One set of five repetitions and one set of two repetitions on the deadlift. Three sets of three bench presses. Repeat every second day (Tsatsouline, 2000).

At first I was skeptical but after just two weeks, I was amazed. Not only was I getting stronger at a ridiculous pace, but the best part was that I had plenty of energy to skateboard. I was never exhausted or too tired to do what I loved most. Simplicity and consistency are the keys to strength.

THE 24 ESSENTIAL EXERCISES FOR ULTIMATE FITNESS

1. Bodyweight Squat—Keep good form, back straight, head up, and squat down as far as you can with weight on your heels and then stand back up

2. Lunge—Step out into a lunge position with your front leg bent at 90 degrees and your back leg straight then step back and repeat with the other leg

3. Jumping Lunges—Get into a lunge position with your front leg bent at 90 degrees and your back leg straight out. Jump into the air while switching your legs and repeat

4. Burpees—Begin standing normally then bend your legs and put your hands on the floor while kicking your feet behind you so that you are in a pushup position. Now bring your knees back into your chest and explode up into a jump

5. Mountain Climbers—Get into a pushup position and begin by bringing one leg close to your arms while the other is outstretched behind you then switch your legs

6. Running on the spot with high knees

7. Sit Ups

8. Plank—Get into a pushup position then use your forearms to support your bodyweight and hold for as long as possible

9. Side Plank—Start on your side or from a normal plank position then put your weight onto your forearm and roll to the side so that you're supporting yourself with the outside of your bottom foot as the base and your forearm at the top

10. Side Sit Up

11. Seated Row—Sit on the floor and extend your legs in front of you using your arms for balance, then bring your legs back into the seated position and repeat the motion

12. Bicycle—Lay on the floor and pretend you're on a bicycle while kicking your legs and rotating your body as if you were doing crunches

13. Flutter Kicks—Lay on the floor body outstretched, now lift your feet 6 to 12 inches off the ground and begin kicking them as if you were swimming. You can also move your feet in a horizontal motion crossing the feet over one another

14. Explosive Jumps—Squat all the way down and explode up as high as you can

15. Tuck Jumps—Jump off your toes rapidly bringing your knees as high up and into your chest as possible

16. One-Legged Squat—Stick one leg out in front of you and proceed to bend your supporting leg into a squat position, try and get as low as possible, and stand back up

17. Wall Sit—Sit with your back against the wall and legs bent at 90 degrees, hold for a duration of time or as long as possible

18. Pushups

19. V-Sit—Sit down and raise your legs about a foot off the ground and use your arms for balance, hold this position for as long as possible. To increase difficulty, raise your feet higher off the ground

20. High Knee Rapid Jumps—Jump and focus on bringing your knees as high into your chest as possible and as fast as possible

21. Jumping Jacks

22. Mason Twist—sit down and clasp your hands together in front of you, now twist from side to side rapidly bringing your arms from one side of your body to the next

23. Frog Jumps—Begin in a deep squat and then explode out as if you were doing a standing long jump but when you land repeat the process

24. One-Legged Jumps—Stand on one leg and begin hopping, focusing on exploding as far as you can with each step

These are all exercises you can do at home without any equipment. Each exercise will develop muscles that will aid an athlete in any sport. Adding the exercises to your daily routine couldn't be easier, all you need to do is choose a few exercises and decide how many repetitions and sets you would like to do. For example you can choose 15, 30, 45, and 60-second intervals and then decide if you'd like to go through the process 1, 2, 3, 4, 5 times or more, which would be the number of sets, here are some concrete examples of workouts.

FOUR KILLER HOME WORKOUTS THAT WILL EXPLODE YOUR ATHLETIC PERFORMANCE

Workout #1
Perform three sets with 25 reps for each exercise

1. Sit Ups
2. Body Weight Squats
3. Pushups
4. Lunges
5. Burpees

Workout #2
Perform three sets of 15 reps for each exercise

1. Explosive Jumps
2. Sit Ups

3. High Knee Rapid Jumps
4. Pushups

Workout #3

Perform three sets of 30-second intervals for each exercise as fast as you can.

1. Pushups
2. Sit Ups
3. Wall Sit
4. V-Sit

Workout #4

Perform each exercise as fast as you can for 30 seconds with no rest between reps and a one minute rest between sets. Perform three sets. This workout is similar to one I learned from my boxing coach who is a two-time Golden Glove champion. I modified it slightly for more explosive power.

1. Body Weight Squats
2. Pushups
3. Sit Ups
4. Flutter Kicks
5. Burpees
6. Bicycle

EVERYTHING YOU NEED TO BUILD THE ULTIMATE HOME GYM THAT IS GUARANTEED TO GIVE YOU ELITE-LEVEL FITNESS FOR DIRT CHEAP

Building a home gym these days couldn't be easier. All you need is a little bit of space to store some small pieces of equipment and some room to move around. You can turn a spare room into a workout space or use the garage, however with modern equipment you do not require that much space only the dedication to actually use the equipment!

TRX Suspension System

With a market saturated with fitness experts and wonder equipment there is one piece of equipment that lives up to the hype and is absolutely perfect for extreme sports athletes because it builds immense core strength, flexibility, and functional strength. The TRX suspension training system is pure gold when it comes to functional strength and it's endorsed and used in nearly all sports including professional hockey, basketball, football, and MMA. The TRX engages the entire body in nearly every single exercise and certainly improves your balance dramatically. The TRX will work out every single muscle.

Figure 21.
The TRX ensures a full body workout and increases stability, strength and balance

Best Exercises to do with the TRX:

- Crunch
- Full Body Roll Out
- One-Legged Burpee
- One Leg Squats
- Jump Squats
- Lateral Lunges
- I-Lunges
- Full Body Rotations

- Incline Row
- V-Ups
- Plank
- Side Plank
- Reverse Plank
- Mountain Climbers
- Pull Up
- Sprinter Starts

Kettlebell

The second piece of equipment, the kettlebell, is excellent for a total body workout as well and is extremely versatile. The kettlebell's popularity has sky rocketed over the last few years because it works the entire body and gets results.

Figure 22.
The kettlebell is the ultimate tool for functional strength and power.

Best exercises to do with the kettlebell:

- Swing
- Deadlift
- One arm swing
- Snatch
- Turkish getups
- Russian twists
- Lunges
- Side Lunges
- Press

Kettelebell Strength Hack:

Pavel Tsatsouline is a Russian strength expert responsible for popularizing the kettlebell in the west. He has written many books on how to most effectively use the kettlebell, such as Enter the Kettlebell, and

Kettlebell Simple and Sinister. The following is his simplest and most effective strategy. Do not underestimate the power of its simplicity. It is extremely effective.

- 10 sets of 10 one arm swings as heavy as you can with good form
- 10 Turkish getups

Do this routine everyday and watch yourself turn into a beast!

Pull-up Bar

The third piece of the puzzle, which is extremely simple and can build immense strength is a simple pull-up bar. There are tons of workouts you can do, and it helps to build next-level core strength and stability.

Figure 23.
Pull ups are simple and effective for full body strength.

Best exercises to do with the pull-up bar:
- Pull Ups
- Back Pull Ups
- Knees to Elbows
- L-Hang
- Toes to Bar
- Knees to Elbows
- Windshield Wiper

Yoga Mat

Finally grab yourself a yoga mat so you don't have any excuses not to get down and work on your core and do HIIT or cardio circuit training. This is simply choosing a few exercises, such as sit-ups, plank, etc. and doing them for bursts of time between 20-60 seconds each.

Best Exercises to do with a yoga mat:
- HIIT Training/Circuit Training
- Yoga
- Stretching
- Abdominal workouts

EXERCISES

Here are a few examples of my favorite exercises. You can add any of these to a workout very easily by doing as many as you can for time or repetitions.

Three Circuits to Give You a Shredded Six Pack

The core is the most important muscle group to develop to help you become an elite athlete because it helps with balance, power, and rotation. Besides that it doesn't hurt to have a shredded six pack to show off to all the people at the beach. When you perform the following circuit five times per week in a very short time you're going to develop an insanely strong core and ripped abs.

Workout Overview

Complete as many repetitions of each exercise as you can for 30 seconds each.

- **Beginner Level:** 3 Rounds
- **Intermediate:** 5 Rounds
- **Advanced:** 8 Rounds
- **World Class Athlete:** 10+ Rounds

Circuit #1

1. Sit Ups with Rotation
2. Seated Row
3. Plank (hold for 30 seconds)
4. Side Plank

5. Side Plank (other side)

6. Scissor Kicks

7. Bicycle

8. Mountain Climbers

Circuit #2

1. One Leg Toe Touches

2. One Leg Toe Touches (other side)

3. Side Crunch

4. Side Crunch (other side)

5. Seated Row

6. Russian Twist

7. Overhead Sit Ups (bringing elbows to knee)

8. Plank

Circuit #3

1. V-Ups

2. Mountain Climbers

3. Seated Row

4. Bicycle

5. Plank

6. Scissor Kicks

7. Russian Twist

8. Mountain Climbers

No man has the right to be an amateur in the matter of physical training. It is a shame for a man to grow old without seeing the beauty and strength of which his body is capable.

— Socrates

The Ultimate Circuit for Developing Pop and Spinning Power

The following is a custom circuit specifically designed to help you hit jumps better, create more spinning and rotational power, and make you spin like a top.

Workout Overview

Complete as many repetitions of each exercise as you can in 15 seconds.

- **Beginner Level**: 2 Circuits
- **Intermediate:** 3-4 Circuits
- **Advanced**: 5+ Circuits

Circuit for Jumping, Popping, and Exploding Rotational Power

1. Jumping 180s
2. Jumping 360s
3. Plank
4. Jumping Knees to Chest
5. Running on the Spot High Knees
6. Jumping Jacks
7. Stationary Explosive Calf Jumps
8. Mountain Climbers

Fitness really can be that simple. If you think these workouts are easy, you'd be mistaken. Not only will doing these workouts give you explosive power and strength, you will gain a very flexible and functional strength that you can apply anywhere. If you were to use only the workouts in this chapter for your entire life, it would probably be all you need to have an insanely high level of fitness and have a ripped body that impresses everyone at the beach, which is a nice bonus.

If you decide to add a training regimen to your routine, you will have a big advantage over other athletes. Having good flexibility, conditioning, and body awareness will translate into better athletic skill. Keep your training simple by taking steps to eat right, stretch, and exercise daily.

Complete This Challenge

The most valuable thing you can do to begin eating healthier and understanding the true power of food is to begin learning about what you're eating. By looking at the ingredients of everything you eat you'll quickly realize how many chemicals, sugars, and unwanted ingredients you're ingesting every day without even realizing it. A simple way to begin eating healthy is to purchase whole, natural foods and cut out as much processed, canned, and ready-made food as you can.

Your challenge for the nutrition component is to start reading the ingredients in everything you buy including sauces like ketchup or hot sauce and packaged and processed foods. Look up the ingredients you can't identify and you may be shocked. The next step is to begin looking for ways to make healthier meals by using whole ingredients. Even the smallest amount of effort and awareness can drastically change your eating habits, which will positively affect your energy levels, health, and mental processes.

Like almost anything in life, consistency is a major key to success. Your challenge for the fitness component is to do one round or more of circuit training for five consecutive days. You can use some of the examples in this chapter to get started or use the list to create your own workouts. The important thing is to make sure you are able to do a minimum of one circuit daily. When you get to the point of being able to complete three circuits at 100 percent twice a day, you will find you have reached a surprisingly high level of fitness.

PLANNING AND GOAL SETTING

*Our goals can only be reached through a
vehicle of a plan, in which we must fervently
believe, and upon which we must vigorously
act. There is no other route to success.*

—Picasso

HOW TO UTILIZE THE POWER OF GOAL SETTING

Extreme sports for the most part are solo sports, meaning you're not required to practice with your team and work on fundamentals like in traditional sports such as football or hockey. When you are a member of a traditional sports team you learn the value of discipline, hard work, and perfecting the details and fundamentals of your craft. The truth of the matter is that there are very few extreme sports athletes who have the dedication to set goals, make a plan, and follow it through. If you apply the information in this component it will be like having a permanent turbo charger for your progression.

When I was running snowboard camps at Snow Park in New Zealand, I used the following process to help riders identify what specifically they wanted from camp, what tricks they wanted to learn, and what they wanted to accomplish. Following this process allows you to make clear goals, and then you can make a definite plan to reach them. The cold hard truth is that your level of athletic skill and ability boils down to you and your hard work. I am about to reveal to you a foolproof process that will allow you to effortlessly uncover your goals and give you a clear path to achieve them. It is extremely important, however, to first know yourself completely and identify your strengths and weaknesses. The easy-to-use chart in Figure 25 will give you a clear understanding of where you are now and what you need to do to get where you want to be.

THE POWER OF KNOWING YOURSELF: YOUR PERSONAL ATHLETIC ASSESSMENT

This self-assessment is designed to give you a quick overview of your strengths and weaknesses. Simply rate yourself between 1 and 10 for each section with 10 indicating you have high level of skill or development and 1 signifying a low skill level that needs work or improvement.

I have included an example assessment sheet for an athlete called Peter that you can use as a reference. It is broken up into three sections fitness, current technical ability, and mental fortitude. Analyze your sport and come up with a list of technical skills and then rate yourself with a score between 1and 10. This will allow you to identify your weaknesses and strengths to become an all-around athlete. For example if you were a skier you could break it up into, rails, jumps, backcountry. If you were a mixed martial artist you could break it down into boxing, jiu-jitsu, wrestling, and so on.

Sample Personal Assessment Worksheet

Fitness Levels	Score
Leg Strength	6
Core Strength	8
Cardio	9
Flexibility	3
Overall Fitness	7

Notes: My biggest weakness is flexibility, especially my hamstrings. My core strength is good from playing sports; however, I could also use a bit more leg strength to give me more stability on the board for flat landings and cliff drops.

Technical Ability	Score

Notes:

Mental Fortitude	Score
Ability to Visualize	7
Ability to Handle Fear	4
Ability to Get in the Zone	7

Ability to Analyze Own Riding and Learn From Mistakes	9
Ability to Make Plans and Record Progress	6
Ability to Concentrate and Focus	6
Overall Mental Strength	7

Notes: I can visualize my tricks quite easily and can see myself doing them perfectly. I struggle with staying confident when learning new tricks or trying something with high consequences because I get nervous. I do my sport as much as I can but don't really plan training times. I can concentrate when I'm interested, but overall I think my mental game is OK. I can see that practicing visualization and using the tools in the confidence component can help me get over my fear and ride more confidently.

Figure 24.
We can learn a great deal about Peter by viewing his self-assessment.

In the example in Figure 24, you can get a clear idea of where Peter is at with his sport. You can easily see his biggest weaknesses and greatest strengths. When you clearly identify where you are then you can make a specific plan to speed up your progression. Fill in the following blank assessments and be as detailed as you like in the notes section.

Your Personal Assessment Worksheet	
Fitness Levels	**Score**
Leg Strength	
Core Strength	
Cardio	
Flexibility	
Overall Fitness	
Notes:	

Technical Ability	Score
(Fill in the blanks with technical skills relevant to your sport.)	
Notes:	
Mental Fortitude	**Score**

Ability to Visualize	
Ability to Handle Fear	
Ability to Get in the Zone	
Ability to Analyze Own Riding and Learn From Mistakes	
Ability to Make Plans and Record Progress	
Ability to Concentrate and Focus	
Overall Mental Strength	
Notes:	

Figure 25.

Performing a self-assessment can identify strengths and weaknesses.

HOW TO EFFECTIVELY SET, MEET, AND SHATTER YOUR GOALS BY MASTERING THE SMART SYSTEM

In a fast paced modern society where distractions are as common as breathing, the ability to learn how to effectively set clear goals can be one of your most powerful tools for success. Goal setting allows you to clearly define what is most important to you and provides the necessary information to develop an action plan. The plan will allow you to stay focused in on what matters most so that every day you will get closer and closer to achieving your dreams. There are libraries full of information on mastering goal setting and in a few paragraphs you're going to learn the strategy that has stood the test of time and is utilized most by successful business people and entrepreneurs today: the SMART system. The SMART system of goal setting was created by Peter Drucker (1954), and it is still widely considered the most concise and effective tool on the subject today.

Specific

The first step is to get very specific about your goals. Begin by asking yourself the five Ws: who, what, where, when, and why.

- Who can help me?
- What do I need to do?
- Where do I need to go?
- When do I have to accomplish certain things?
- Why do I want to achieve this goal?

It is much more powerful to set specific goals such as, "I want to master the backflip." When you are specific then you have a precise target to aim for. Avoid vague goals such as "I want to be awesome at my sport."

Measurable

The second part is to ensure that you have a definite and measurable way to recognize your progress. This can be tricks you're trying to learn, hitting your goals for dry land and fitness training, or anything else as long as you can measure it. This is where keeping a log or journal of your training will come in extra handy as you can record daily, weekly, and monthly progress, which will motivate you and keep you on track.

Achievable

Be sure your goals are achievable. This is where you sit down and give yourself a reality check and test your dedication. Once your goals are written, sit down and ask yourself:

- Am I prepared to make the commitment to reach this goal?
- Am I willing to change aspects of my life to make these goals a reality?
- Is this something I truly want and will work to achieve in the days, weeks, and months to come?

When you identify goals that are important to you then you can develop the beliefs, skills, and abilities to reach them. Remember that you want to set the bar high but be reasonable about your current abilities or time frame to achieve them. If you want to learn a double-backflip but can't do a backflip yet, then accomplish that first and move forward from there. Give yourself the necessary time to hit your big goals.

Relevant

The fourth criterion points out the importance of choosing goals that matter. Be sure your goals are relevant to your desired outcome. Some questions you want to ask yourself during this stage of the model are:

- Is this goal worth my time?
- Is this goal worth my effort?
- Is this goal something I really want to accomplish?

This is where you make sure that the goal is going to be something that you truly want to accomplish and decide if it's relevant to you and worth the effort.

Time-bound

The fifth and final criterion in the SMART model stresses the importance of giving your goals a timeline. It is important to give yourself a realistic deadline to complete your goals so that they create a certain internal pressure to accomplish the goals within the given time frame. Most people, without a date or time to accomplish a task, will continue to put it on the back burner, saving it for another day. I'm sure most of you know this to be true if you're in school or remember what it was like to do a school project. Some questions to consider in this step:

- When can this goal be completed?
- What can I do today to reach my goal?
- What can I do two weeks from now?
- What can I do three months from now?

Giving your goal a deadline will create a sense of urgency and increase the likelihood of you achieving it.

The SMART model is a simple and powerful tool you can use to set goals in your athletic and personal life. As you sit down and decide what you want to accomplish in your life go through the process and ensure you're making your goal-setting process as effective as possible.

The significance of a man is not in what he attains but what he longs to attain.

— Kahlil Gibran

HOW TO EASILY DEFINE AND SET CLEAR GOALS

The first step to goal setting is to come up with a list of all the things you'd like to achieve in athletics, both big and small. A common interest I find among young athletes is that they all want to go pro but what most of them really want is to immerse themselves in their sport. Most people have no idea what the life of a pro athlete is like, and many people manage to do their sport every day in different ways and have even more freedom than a pro. That being said let's create a list of goals an athlete might have.

Goals

- I want to learn to execute a backflip.
- I want to be a pro athlete.
- I want to do my sport every single day.
- I want to win my local contest.
- I want to learn ten new tricks this year.
- I want the best equipment.
- I want to travel around the world competing in my sport.
- I want to get sponsored.
- I want to get lots of good footage of me performing my sport.
- I want to make a mini movie of my friends and myself performing our sport.
- I want to take a road trip this season to (X) to compete in my sport.
- I want to perform my best during contests and win every one I enter.

HOW TO MAKE A CLEAR AND STRUCTURED PLAN TO LAUNCH YOU AS IF FROM A CATAPULT TO ACHIEVE AND SURPASS YOUR GOALS

Now that you have made your goals clear and tangible, it's time to formulate a plan to achieve them. Begin with the smaller goals like learning a trick that is within your ability. If your big goal is to go pro then it is important to give yourself a realistic timeline to get there. Furthermore, if your goal is to be a pro athlete your midterm goal should be to create a life where you can do your sport every day.

You can use this process for learning new tricks quickly, for example, if you want to learn a specific move you can begin by trying to create simulation training for that move; study the move by watching others; and continually visualize the move or trick you're trying to learn. You can repeat this process for anything you're trying to learn by scheduling dry land training, mental training, and specific practice times.

The next step is to ensure you have an effective training program to achieve your big goals. The more dedicated you are to your training, the more results you're going to see. Figure 26 is a sample weeklong training program that is quite similar to what I give to my national team athletes, pro-boarders, and camp students. Once the goals are set in place we focus on specific dry land training every morning and visualizing tricks every night; we also ensure that all-around skills are being developed through time at the gym, yoga, gymnastics, and on the trampoline. We make use of all of the resources we have available, and when you create your own plan you can do the same.

THE POWER OF STICKING TO A PLAN AND RECORDING PROGRESS

Once you have decided what your goals are and made a clear plan of action, you must follow through! Acting on your plan is the most essential step and having the discipline to follow through with your training is what is going to separate you from the rest of the pack. It's the difference between day dreaming and living your dreams and between a hopeless dreamer and an elite-level athlete.

After a few short weeks of actually training effectively most of my students are downright shocked at the progress they are able to make. It's important to go out and buy a notebook that is only for your athletic training and log everything. Write down your goals, your training schedule, and at the end of every day and every week record what you actually did, what worked well, what was easy, what was difficult, and what breakthroughs you had. After a season you'll look back in amazement at how much you were able to accomplish when you follow through and apply proper training to your sport. The log will give you motivation, proof your training is working, and added determination to continue accomplishing your goals. *Remember to plan daily, weekly, and monthly* to keep your vision strong, clear, and concise.

Figure 28.
Have a dedicated journal to record your goals and accomplishments

Our plans miscarry because they have no aim. When a man does not know what harbor he is making for, no wind is the right wind.

— Seneca

High Impact Sample Training Plan

	Sunday	Monday	Tuesday	Wednesday	Thursday	Friday	Saturday
7:00 am	Wake Up	Wake Up	Wake Up	Wake Up	Wake Up	Wake Up	Wake Up
:30	Breakfast	Breakfast	Breakfast	Breakfast	Breakfast	Breakfast	Breakfast
8:00 am	Dry land training	Dry land training	Dry land training	Dry land training	Dry land training	Dry land training	Dry land training
:30	Sport	Sport	Sport	Sport	Sport	Sport	Sport
10:00 am	Sport	Sport	Sport	Sport	Sport	Sport	Sport
11:00 am							
12:00 am	Sport	Sport	Sport	Sport	Sport	Sport	Sport
1:00 pm							
2:00 pm	Sport	Sport	Sport	Sport	Sport	Sport Morning ONLY	Sport
:30						REST	
3:00 pm							
3:30						20 Minute Visualization Practice	

	Sunday	Monday	Tuesday	Wednesday	Thursday	Friday	Saturday
4:00 pm	Sport	Sport	Sport	Sport	Sport		Sport
5:00 pm							
6:00	Dryland Training	Yoga	Trampoline Practice 1.5 hours	Gymnastics	Yoga		Dryland training
7:00 pm	Workout						Workout
8:00	20 Minute Stretch	20 Minute Visualization Practice	20 Minute Stretch	20 Minute Visualization Practice	20 Minute Visualization Practice	20 Minute Visualization Practice	
9:00 pm	15 Minute Visualization Practice		20 Minute Visualization Practice				20 Minute Visualization Practice

Figure 26.
A sample weeklong training program.

My Weekly Training Plan

	Sunday	Monday	Tuesday	Wednesday	Thursday	Friday	Saturday
7:00 am							
:30							
8:00 am							
:30							
10:00 am							
11:00 am							
12:00 am							
1:00 pm							
2:00 pm							

:30							
3:00 pm							
3:30							
4:00 pm							
5:00 pm							
6:00							
7:00 pm							
8:00							
9:00 pm							

Figure 27.
Use this table to make your own weekly training plan.

Many great minds have expressed the belief that excellence is a habit not a single action. Setting goals and making a plan to achieve them is a simple process; however, most choose to ignore it and miss out on harnessing its significant power. When you set clearly defined goals and carve out a path to achieve them you are dedicating yourself to your progression and you will be thrilled with the results. As you begin achieving your goals one by one you will feel the joy of setting new and bigger goals!

Complete This Challenge

Your challenge for the planning and goal setting component is going to require you take action and formulate a plan. Do not read another word until you've completed this challenge because it is going to give you a platform to achieve your goals and give you a great deal of confidence. You'll see that with a little hard work you can make your goals a reality.

1. Make a giant list of all your athletic goals, big and small.

2. Go through the SMART model and ensure your goals are congruent with what you want to accomplish.

3. Write out a rough timeline of where you'd like to be as far as progressing towards your goals in the coming days, weeks, months, and years. For example, "This week I will start specific training for learning backflips and start practicing visualization. In a few months I'd like to be able to do backflips and begin winning contests. Next year I hope to be sponsored and compete more often. In two years I will make a life out of my sport and do all of things I see pros doing now."

4. Use the training plan template and create this week's first training schedule and continue to plan your weeks so that you can effectively manage your time to accomplish your goals.

ZEN AND THE
ART OF ATHLETICS

*All that we are is the result
of what we have thought.*
—Buddha

FIND YOUR CENTER AND EXPERIENCE ZEN

There lives inside of us a place of peace, joy, compassion, and infinite possibility. Most people go through life without ever truly understanding who they are, what they want, or even come close to fulfilling their full potential. Each one of us *are* the creators of our own reality and must take responsibility for how we feel, how we act, and what we will achieve in our lives. Have you ever wondered why some people with seemingly no skill or talent are happy and wildly successful while others who seem to have natural ability can't seem to catch a break? There are laws that govern this universe, and I will reveal to you the secret to being happier, achieving what you want in life, and how to become the greatest athlete possible, and make your wildest dreams come true. Before I expose this timeless secret I must first tell you a true story.

There is a man who lives in a temple high up in the Kunya Mountains in China with the ability to break two-inch concrete slabs with just two fingers. He can stab his index finger through a glass window leaving only the hole in the glass as evidence. The man's name is Master Guo, and he is a Shaolin Kung Fu Master and master of Qi Gong (energy), and these are just a few of the unbelievable physical feats he is able to accomplish. As a student at the Shaolin Academy in 2013 I had the pleasure of training under Master Guo and learned several timeless lessons that I will pass on to you. We sat in his office at the academy with traditional martial art and Chinese décor surrounding us. He is a very small man, about 5 feet 6 inches tall and weighs about 120 pounds soaking wet, with a very calm and friendly demeanor. The translator, "Elle" as the students called her, sat at our right so that we could communicate because none of the masters at the academy speak English.

Figure 29.
For years, students and masters of Qi Gong have practiced by striking trees at the academy. Some of the indentions are half an inch deep.

I began with a few simple questions, and Master Guo gave me a brief overview of his entire life and what brought him to martial arts and the study of Qi Gong. My goal of the interview was to find out how I could harness this incredible mental power that he had and share it with others. I was looking for a way to somehow invoke his incredible abilities, and at the end of this interview I knew two incredibly significant truths. When I would question the master about how it was possible to do seemingly impossible feats he simply smiled and started striking the desk with his index finger so hard it sounded like he was hitting it with a hammer and said, "Years." He then stopped and pointed at his head and said, "Years." He was clearly implying it was achieved through years of conditioning his fingers and his mind. I continued to question further only to realize that the master thinks of his abilities, as he put it, as "nothing special," and he believes that *everyone has this power.* I learned that he spent much of his life whole-heartedly dedicated to one simple thing—martial arts. The master practices hard Qi Gong daily. The evidence of this can be found on the trees at the academy where students and masters alike strike the trees with just their fingers, fists, and elbows. After many years there are visible imprints upon the trees, many of which are half an inch deep!

The master has been practicing energy work or Qi Gong for most of his life and has developed extraordinary physical and mental abilities. The master told me many stories as I continued to try and extract some tips, tools, or practices that could put me on the fast track to achieving just a trace of his abilities. The conversation lasted an hour but felt like only minutes since I was hanging on his every word. When the interview concluded I sincerely thanked the master for his time and wisdom.

It wasn't until a few days later that I fully understood the true power of what I learned, witnessed, and experienced at the academy. My entire life I have looked for the technique, way, answer, or secret to everything from being as strong as possible, faster, smarter, richer, more enlightened to being able to achieve my dreams, understand the purpose and meaning of life, and what's possible and more. I have been on the constant search for the one truth, the way to achieve superhuman abilities both physically and mentally. This search led me to Nepal where I trekked Mt. Everest and meditated with monks for 30 days, to Thailand where I trained with some of the world's best MMA fighters, and finally to China to learn the secrets of the Shaolin monks.

The lessons I learned from Master Guo were both humbling and remarkable. The real secret to achieving superhuman strength, achieving your dreams, having extraordinary mind power is... *there is no secret!* There is no short cut! I know right now you're feeling like you got ripped off but stay with me because the secrets only have value if you're operating under this fundamental truth. You see my whole life I was looking for the easy way, the fast way, the short cut. This was hard for me to deal with considering I had been travelling around the world to find these secrets; however, almost immediately after I accepted that truth I came to understand another fundamental truth: a*nything is possible with persistence and discipline.*

Figure 30.
Master Guo and Matthew Belair at the Shaolin Academy.

A common thread in Zen literature refers to levels of understanding, meaning your ability to understand a lesson more deeply, to understand its essence. Although I knew the fundamental truths Master Guo spoke of, to see the power of them when applied literally transformed my understanding and belief in the concepts. Master Guo spent years developing his abilities day in and day out. His job was to train in martial arts, and after years of discipline and dedication he is now able to do things that most people believe to be impossible. It is important to realize that he doesn't see his ability as anything special because he put in the work, he believed in himself, and he knew it could be done.

The secret that anything is possible with belief and dedication is so simple most will fail to harness its true power; however, remember almost all ground-breaking discoveries are simple; look at the wheel for example. In today's world everyone is looking for a short cut, they want abs while eating chips and watching television. Everyone wants something for nothing; few are willing to put in the hard work necessary to do what it takes to achieve their goals.

The liberating truth that I learned from my time with Master Guo and the other Sifus is that when you have the discipline to continuously look within and try to understand yourself, understand your own mind, understand your energy, power, and potential, literally anything is possible. With the same dedication to any idea that Master Guo put towards developing the strength of his fingers and strength of mind to break concrete you can literally achieve anything! The Shaolin masters are living proof that if you have a goal or dream and you dedicate yourself 100 percent to that dream then it is not only possible it is inevitable. Shaolin monks are truly exceptional examples of how to train your body to achieve its maximum potential. They bring the mind and body together every day in training and can perform mind-blowing feats of strength, speed, and agility. I'm curious if you're starting to understand that when you apply even a fraction of their training method and dedication there's no telling what you can achieve whether it's in sport or life.

HOW TO REACH ENLIGHTENMENT: THE REAL-LIFE STORY OF AN ENLIGHTENED MASTER

The concept of enlightenment has been one that has consumed me for years and is wrapped in mystery, misdirection, simplicity, and confusion all at once. When you immerse yourself in the literature of achieving enlightenment, or nirvana, you begin to realize there are some fundamental themes that continually arise such as enlightenment is here and now, you do not have to search for enlightenment, you cannot grasp or hold onto enlightenment, let go and it will find you, and many more riddles. I had been on the path for years, and all of the riddles and stories remained a mystery until I began to receive extremely clear insights during deep meditations, dreams, and through a conversation with an enlightened master.

I knew humans were capable of incredible things, and I knew that the power of the mind is infinite, and there is a way to inner peace and connection. This is what drove me to travel the world to find the people with the answers and had no idea there was a master at my doorstep. I met an incredible human being in the winter of 2014 I will call John because my friend prefers anonymity. I instantly knew there was something special about him. I only met him in passing a few times before we decided to hang out one day in my home in Vernon, British Columbia, Canada. I was living in a beautiful house on the water, snowboarding and meditating daily. As we were having a deep conversation about life, the universe, meditation, and other deep subjects his knowledge was so profound and clear it was shocking. And then it hit me: he was fully awake; he was an enlightened master. This does not mean he could float around or do anything weird; it means that he could see the truth.

John's ego (perception of oneself as separate; the conscious mind of "I") was non-existent, and he had clear vision. When I made this realization he told me that to get to this state he was willing to give up everything and stay in meditation for the rest of his life until he found the answer. He had been on the journey to awakening most of his life and decided it was time to dedicate completely and sat in meditation for 20 hours a day for 100 days before he had his awakening. John described it as a bolt of lightning rushing through his body, as he was gifted a clear vision of this reality. You may find this to be unbelievable, and that's OK; however, many others have had similar experiences such as Eckhart Tolle, the author of *The Power of Now* (1997), who had his awakening after years of depression and suffering. He sat in his room one night ready to end his life when he said to himself, "I can't live with myself anymore," and instantly his awakening occurred! He realized the duality in his thought, "*I* can't live with *myself* anymore." Who is I? Why are there two? And yet another common theme of enlightenment and Zen arises within the duality.

Realize deeply that the present moment is all you have. Make the NOW the primary focus of your life.

—*Eckhart Tolle*

In order to wake up and realize the truth you must realize there is no "I" or "me." So what are you then? You simply *are*. You *are awareness*. Enlightenment is that feeling you get when you lose yourself in your sport, and you're completely free of all thoughts, and you're fully immersed in the moment, and you are simply *being* and fully present. When you're in this state of mind it is easier to realize that you are not your arm or your body; if you lose a leg you're still *you*. *You* are not your thoughts or consciousness because that changes in an instant. You must go beyond the conscious rational mind to know who you really *are*. Therein lies the difficulty of explaining it to the rational mind, and so the creation of Zen poems, riddles, and seemingly end-less contradictory stories ascended from masters and teachers.

John and I went on to discuss many subjects, and he spoke with a level of depth and truth that was obviously from a place of real understanding. Through my own practices I have had more than a few glimpses into this clear insight, enlightenment, or awakened mindset, which allowed me the ability to spot it in another.

So what is the point? What is the lesson? How do we achieve this state of clarity and inner peace? The truth of the matter is that the path is different for each and every one of us, we are all unique and special, and honoring ourselves is the first principle. It is to align yourself with what feels right and to continually break down the illu-sions of the mind. The more you can bring yourself into mindfulness, the moment, the present, the more clarity you will begin to develop because everything else is simply a trick of the mind. In your ear-nest seeking you will begin to discover the truth and wisdom within yourself.

It is painfully obvious to me that most of you reading this book will certainly not believe the above story to be true or have any idea what I'm talking about. That's OK, the point isn't to make you believe or disbelieve anything. My hope is that you take the story as a seed to start looking within, to find your own answers, to find your place of peace and *real* knowing. The mind is a powerful thing, and with modern technology we are bombarded relentlessly with brainwashing and distraction. To have the discipline to look within and discover the power of your true self is no easy task; however, when facing our end, as we all inevitably will, the task of knowing oneself is the only worthy task to undertake.

19 POWERFUL QUESTIONS TO UNCOVER WHO YOU TRULY ARE

- What am I most passionate about?
- What interests me most?
- What would I do for free?
- If I could do anything and knew I could not fail what would it be?
- What do I value most?
- What am I most grateful for?
- What qualities do I value most in a person?
- What makes me happiest?
- What people, places, and circumstances give me the most joy?
- What is my dream?

- What is my passion?
- What is my purpose?
- What is my mission?
- What does my perfect life look like?
- What do I need to be truly free?
- How do I want to feel at every moment of every day?
- What people, places, experiences cause me to feel that way naturally?
- What prevents those experiences and feelings?
- What can I do to have those experiences and feelings more often?

ESSENTIAL PRINCIPLES FOR ACHIEVING INNER PEACE AND LIVING A HAPPIER LIFE

- Live in the moment as much as you can. It is all there is, was, and ever will be.
- Let go of anger.
- Let go of judgment.
- Let go of fear.
- Let go of comparing.
- Let go of regrets.
- Let go of blame.
- Let go of worrying.
- Identify your values.
- Appreciate your life and show gratitude.

- Simplify your life.
- Show compassion.
- Seek truth.
- Trust yourself and develop your intuition.
- Be kind to yourself and others.
- Discover what inspires you.
- Uncover your principles and code, and live by it.
- Follow your heart.
- Separation is an illusion; you are never alone; we are all one.
- Don't stress about things you cannot change; do not worry about the future; do not live in regret; be here now.

THE THREE MOST FUNDAMENTAL ZEN TEACHINGS THAT CAN CHANGE YOUR LIFE

Although achieving things in life is great, Zen is so much more than being able to accomplish superhuman feats, become a pro athlete, or accomplish your dreams. Zen is the journey; it's a feeling, an understanding, a perspective that allows you to experience total freedom. Zen is the feeling you have when you're completely immersed in your sport and nothing else is on your mind (no mind); you are completely at one with yourself, your board, the mountain; and you're totally aware and in the moment. This full awareness is the essence of Zen and through the pursuit of achieving your highest potential in your sport you will learn many lessons about yourself along the way.

To become great at anything requires a certain mindset, understanding, and discipline. However, Zen is not about achieving anything; it's in fact quite the opposite. Zen is full awareness, direct insight, and being totally immersed in the moment. There is no goal or outcome to be achieved in Zen, it is rather to be completely and totally satisfied with the here and now; however, humans are born with a natural desire to create, explore, and grow. It is to be commended that you are the type of person to push yourself, to test your limits, and seek growth. These are all attributes to be admired; however, if you simply go through life with the purpose of achieving and gaining things or objects you will ultimately be left empty. Combining the natural inclination to grow as a person with these three attributes of a Zen mind, you will begin formulating an exceptionally empowering mindset. The three fundamental teachings are non-attachment, non-judgment, and non-resistance.

Non-Attachment

Attachment is one of the main causes for suffering in nearly all people. When you free yourself from attachment not only to material objects but to outcomes, people, and circumstances you will gain a newfound sense of total freedom.

The reason many people in our society are miserable, sick, and highly stressed is because of an unhealthy attachment to things they have no control over.

—Steve Maraboli

Almost all suffering is caused by our thinking. Most of us do not take responsibility for how we feel when the truth is that *you* decide how you feel at any given moment. The only thing we truly hold power over is our ability to choose our perspective to any given situation. When you give that power back to yourself and choose not to be a victim, choose a positive perspective, and ultimately *let go* of all of the negative thoughts, feelings, and emotions that are not serving you then you're choosing to empower yourself. This action of letting go will cause you to free your mind from a universe of unnecessary burden. The Zen story of the travelling monks will help solidify this point.

> Two travelling monks reached a river where they met a young woman. Wary of the current, she asked if they could carry her across. One of the monks hesitated, but the other quickly picked her up onto his shoulders, transported her across the water, and put her down on the other bank. She thanked him and departed.
>
> As the monks continued on their way, the other monk was brooding and preoccupied. Unable to hold his silence, he spoke out.
>
> "Brother, our spiritual training teaches us to avoid any contact with women, but you picked that one up on your shoulders and carried her!"
>
> "Brother," the second monk replied, "I set her down on the other side, while you are still carrying her."(Reps, 1957)

The story clearly illustrates how easy it is to become attached to things whether it's a material object, outcome, belief, or even a thought. To be fully present and achieve "no mind" you must rid yourself of all mental attachments and surrender completely to the present moment.

Non-Judgment

It is only natural for humans to judge, label, and categorize everything we see and experience throughout the day. It is very likely that you're doing this far more than you realize. When you are unconsciously programmed to judge everything you see and experience, the result is filling your mind to the brim with unnecessary mental garbage. It is an essential skill in Zen teachings to learn to see things as they are, without labels. It is essential to practice non-judgment in your day-to-day dealings with other people. Each and every person has something to teach us, and many Zen teachers will refer to other people as mirrors for what we need to see, experience, or change within ourselves. If you were to adopt the principle of compassion when dealing with all people throughout your daily interactions you would experience much change. If someone is mad at you, frustrated, or bothering you, consider showing as much love and compassion as you can towards that person, and you will transform your own negative feelings into something positive and give them no power while the other person will still be burdened with their negative energies.

Non-judgment refers to all things we experience such as material objects, outcomes, or experiences. It is believed that when you judge and categorize things you miss their true essence because your mind is working to categorize and place the experience in the "correct box" in your mind rather than being fully present and experiencing things as they really *are*. As your mind is on autopilot you are missing the true nature of the experience. Consider this parable adapted from the story Brother Disciples.

> There is an old Zen story that tells of a master who presents his students with a bowl and asks, "What is this?"
>
> The first student picks up the bowl and starts tapping it with his fingers and turns it into a drum, and the master responds, "Very good."
>
> The next student takes the bowl and wears it on his head like a hat, and again the master says, "Very good."
>
> Finally the last student receives the bowl, and again the master asks, "What is this?" The student examines the bowl for a few moments before hurling it to the ground smashing it into thousands of pieces. The Zen master responds, "Excellent!"

The lesson was in learning to see things as they are and not as we want them to be. A bowl is not just a bowl; the bowl "never was" unless our minds created it, the bowl just is. If you were to learn to see things as they are, allow your mind to be free, and be entirely present within each moment then you will begin to experience these teachings with more depth and understanding. The story of the Zen farmer demonstrates my point.

> Once upon a time there was an old farmer who, for many years, worked on his farm. One day his only horse ran away and when

his neighbors heard the news, they immediately came to visit the farmer and called out, "Such bad luck!"

"Maybe," the old farmer replied.

Not long after, the horse returned again. Not only that, it brought three other wild horses along. "What luck and good fortune!" his neighbors exclaimed.

To which the old farmer replied, "Maybe."

After a while the farmer's son tried to ride one of the wild horses and was thrown by the untamed horse and broke his leg. Again his neighbors came over to convey their concern about their neighbor's bad luck.

"Maybe," said the farmer once again.

A few weeks later some military officials visited the village to draft young men into the army, but since his son's leg was broken, the officials passed him by. The neighbors were surprised how fortunate things had turned out and congratulated the farmer on his good luck, to which he replied, "Maybe." (Watts, 2006)

The wise farmer unlike his neighbors does not judge the event good or bad. He practices non-judgment and therefore avoids the trap of labeling the event in his mind, essentially keeping it empty, clear, and present. The meaning we attach and put on to people, circumstances, events, and situations is always our choice and it is subjective. If you were to look for and always choose the most positive perspective possible in any given situation you would train yourself to be a happier person and your life would improve as a result.

Non-Resistance

As a species, resisting is one of our best traits although it doesn't serve us. We want it to be this way, we want that thing. Every single time we complain we are resisting "what is" and creating mental anguish. Many things in life are within our control and many are not. The wise man is able to recognize the difference between the two and act accordingly.

Non-Resistance is the key to the greatest power in the universe.

—Eckhart Tolle

It is perfectly fine to desire change and to want to create a more ideal circumstance, but it is also important to not resist or reject where you are now. If you want a better environment to progress your abilities you can make it one of your goals, and remember to accept where you are now as part of the journey. The old saying, "It's not the destination, it's the journey," goes hand in hand with non-resistance. Life never was and never will be as perfect or easy as the mind would like; we are all on a ride, and we get to choose how much we enjoy it and how we respond to our circumstances. The more we can accept our realities and roadblocks, while taking action to grow as individuals and fill our life with what makes us happiest without being attached to the outcome, the easier the ride will be. The ancient story of Zen Master Hakuin illustrates my point.

The Zen Master Hakuin was well-known and recognized among his village as one living a pure life.

A beautiful young girl always lived near his house. Suddenly her parents realized that she was pregnant, which made them very mad. But she was afraid and would not confess the father of the child. But since her parents didn't give in, she finally named Master Hakuin.

In great anger the parents went to Hakuin and told him the news of how they knew he was the father. "Is that so?" was his only reply.

Right after the child was born, the parents came to Hakuin and demanded that he fulfill his responsibility as the father and take care of the child. By then the master's upstanding reputation in the village had been tarnished.

"Is that so?" said Hakuin as he calmly accepted the child.

After a year the mother couldn't hold to her lie any longer and confessed to her parents that the young man at the local fish market was the real father.

The parents rushed to Hakuin to apologize and asked for his forgiveness, which he granted. They told him that the child belonged to a local boy who worked at the fish market.

"Is that so?" said Hakuin as he returned the child.

The Zen master practices acceptance or non-resistance to the highest degree. He is fully aware that the child is not his; however, he does not resist the circumstance he is presented. He shows the child love and cares for him knowing there may be a lesson learned from the experience, and when the truth comes to light he is able to return the child back to the rightful father with the same calm acceptance as he had when receiving the child. This story is extreme, but if the Zen master could accept such an intense life changing circumstance, we can only hope to exercise that acceptance when dealing with the inconsequential things in life we put so much effort towards that, in the end, really don't matter at all.

Complete This Challenge

Congratulations you've made it to your final challenge! If you have missed even one challenge from a previous chapter go back and make sure you complete it. This final challenge aims to help you bring about change and know yourself more deeply. Complete the following tasks.

1. Complete all challenges in the book.

2. Answer the 19 Powerful Questions in this chapter

3. What did you find most useful about this book?

4. What brings you the most joy, and how can you experience more of it in your life?

5. Believe in yourself, keep learning, be grateful, and never give up!

FINAL THOUGHTS

Mastering others is strength.
Mastering yourself is true power.
—Lao Tzu

HOW TO AVOID INJURY AND RECOVER LIKE A SUPERHUMAN

The mind is more powerful than you can imagine and when you embody this truth you can allow it to work its natural magic. There are countless studies and people that have proved that the mind can heal the body in profound ways. In his book *You Are the Placebo* (2014) Dr. Joe Dispenza proves beyond a doubt our minds can heal our bodies. One of the best examples is a study done in Japan on children who were allergic to poison ivy. The researchers rubbed one arm with poison ivy and told the kids it was a harmless plant. They rubbed the other arm with a harmless plant and told the kids it was poison ivy. Amazingly their body's reversed the rash! All children developed a rash where the harmless leaf was rubbed, and 11 of the 13 developed no rash where the poison ivy touched them. Welcome to the world of the placebo effect and the power of your mind.

Dr. Joe Dispenza (2014) provides many cases and provides proof about how the placebo effect works in our minds and bodies and how powerful it actually is. Dispenza has been teaching people to use the power of their minds to heal themselves for the last five years and has many documented cases of people curing themselves of disease including cancer, cystic fibrosis, and other diseases. Dispenza believes we are about to make quantum leaps in medicine because when we understand that the mind both creates and eradicates disease we can gain more control over our health through education and direct understanding.

Another startling example involves Henry Beecher, a World War II doctor. During the war supplies began to run low and Beecher ran out of morphine to give the soldiers. Beecher thinking on his feet started giving the soldiers saline injections and telling them it was morphine. To his surprise about 50 percent of the soldiers had their pain eased or completely taken away to the point of being able to cut into flesh to make repairs on the wounded patients. Beecher went on to study the placebo effect and published his ground-breaking findings to the medical field in a 1955 issue of the *Journal of the American Medical Association* (Dispenza, 2014).

Avoiding Injury

Most athletes believe that injury is just a part of the game. This is a fundamental error in thinking if you are to remain healthy. The number one reason why people attract the things they do not want into their lives is because they continually think about and talk about the things they do not want. If you are about to enter a competition, learn a new skill, or try something dangerous what thoughts go through your head? Of course it is possible that you may fall but it is your job to remove that thought from your psyche and focus completely and totally on completing the task at hand. Where you focus your attention is where you focus your energy!

The most effective way to avoid injury is to pay attention to where you focus your energy. The first step is to stop talking about injury, sickness, and illness and focus on health. You may be aware that the people who speak about illness and sickness the most are the ones that have it. Dispenza's placebo theory suggests that our words and thoughts manifest in the body, and we now have the science to prove it so be mindful of your words.

The next step in avoiding injury is to catch your stray thoughts and refocus on what you want. If you are going to try a new trick or something dangerous your mindset should be completely on executing that task perfectly. If you find yourself saying, "I hope I don't fall," Stop and ask yourself, "So what do I want?" And bring your focus back to completing the task at hand. When you completely change your words and thoughts and direct them completely towards what it is that you want, which is being healthy, the mind and body respond.

How to Recover Like a Superhuman

Bruce Lee suffered a severe back injury and was told he would never kick again; however, eight months later he was out of the hospital and better than ever. Dispenza suffered a severe accident and was told he was never going to walk again. He decided he was the creator of his reality and healed his body completely and enjoys walking around with no pain. There are countless stories like these which are here to help you realize how powerful you are. Here are the simple steps to recovering quickly from injury.

The first step is to relax your mind just like in the guided meditations. Once your mind is completely relaxed focus your energy towards the part of you that needs the healing. If your knee is in recovery send healing energy towards your knee. Simply set a mental intention to heal your knee and make your visualization as vivid as possible. Visualize sending healing green light towards your knee as you internally feel yourself healing. Visualize your knee in your mind as strong and healthy. Stay in this space for 30 minutes or longer continuing to send healing energy to yourself.

The next step is to imagine what it is going to feel like once you are completely healthy. Visualize yourself in perfect health. What will it feel like with a healthy, strong knee and body? How does it feel to be completely healed? See yourself running, jumping, exercising, and playing your sport with a powerfully strong body. Finally, at the end of your meditation give gratitude for your healing and surrender your healing to the quantum field with gratitude and expectation that your body is responding.

In the same way that your mouth will begin to water if you imagine biting into a big juicy lemon, your mind will heal your body. There are countless stories of miraculous recovery using the simple process above. Now it's up to you to commit to the practice so you can be added to that list of people!

I promised you at the beginning of the final chapter that I would empower you with the secrets to achieving all that you want in life and it is my hope that you understand the simplicity and power of the lessons presented. Through the process of dedication, believing in yourself, and the realization that there are no short cuts, anything truly is possible. The purpose of this book is to help you to cultivate a strong mind, develop self-discipline, and mental acuity.

The road to excellence, self-discovery, and self-mastery is a long one. It is a journey and lifestyle. You do not wake up one day with all of the answers and the ability to do whatever you'd like in sport; the skill and development come from dedication, and your success is earned, never given. When you clearly define your goals, earnestly try to learn about yourself at the deepest level, and set on a pursuit to achieve your dreams with time, dedication, and belief and you will get there. My hope is that this book has inspired you to apply the concepts within it and furthermore to continue to learn more about yourself and the world.

You now hold in your hands all of the tools I have spent years of researching, experimenting, and travelling to acquire. By simply reading this book you will experience little benefit but with dedication to the practices within, the sky is the limit. *Believe in yourself always!*

WORKS CITED

Innerfire: Extraordinary in Everyone. "Wim Hof." Last Modified 2016. http://www.icemanwimhof.com/wim-hof-iceman-.

Pavlov, Ivan. 1910. *The Work of the Digestive Glands*. London: C. Griffin.

Santarnecchi, E., D'Arista, S., Egiziano, E., Gardi, C., Petrosino, R., Vatti, G., Reda, M. and Alessandro Rossi. 2014. Interaction Between Neuroanatomical and Psychological Changes after Mindfulness-Based Training. *San Francisco: PLOS One.*

Richardson, Alan. "Mental Practice: A Review and Discussion Part 1." Research Quarterly. American Association for Health, Physical Education and Recreation 38 (1967): 95-107. Accessed April, 25, 2016. http://www.tandfonline.com/doi/pdf/10.1080/10671188.19 67.10614808?needAccess=true&redirect=1

Morris, T., Spittle, M., and Anthony Watt. 2005. *Imagery in Sport.* Lower Mitcham: Human Kinetics Publishers.

O'Connor, Joseph. 2001. *NLP and Sports: How to Win the Mind Game.* Toronto: HarperCollins Canada/Thorsons.

Jackson, Phil. 2013. *Eleven Rings: The Soul of Success.* New York: Penguin Books USA.

O'Connor, J., and Ian McDermott. 1996. *Principles of NLP.* London: Thorsons Publishing Group.

Dispenza, Joe. 2014. *You Are the Placebo: Making Your Mind Matter.* Carlsbad: Hay House.

Cunningham, Les. 1984. *Hypnosport: The Creative Use of Hypnosis to Maximize Athletic Performance.* Philadelphia: Richard West.

Institute for Health Metrics and Evaluation. "The State of US Health: Innovations, Insights, and Recommendations from the Global Burden of Disease Study." University of Washington. Last Modified 2010. http://www.healthdata.org/sites/default/files/files/policy_report/2013/USHealth/IHME_GBD_USHealth_FullReport.pdf.

Soundcloud, Belair: Mind & Spirit. "Podcast Episode 7: Transform your Life with the Power of Food with Best Selling Author Adam Hart." Last Modified 2016. https://soundcloud.com/belair-3/transform-your-life-with-the-power-of-food-adam-hart-ep-7.

Tsatsouline, Pavel. 2000. *Power to the People!:Russian Strength Training Secrets for Every American.* Little Canada: Dragon Door Publications.

Tsatsouline, Pavel. 2013. *Kettlebell Simple and Sinister*. Reno: StrongFirst, Inc.

Drucker, Peter. 1954. *The Practice of Management*. New York: Harper & Row.

Tolle, Eckhart. 2004. *The Power of Now: A Guide to Spiritual Enlightenment*. Vancouver: Namaste Publishing.

Reps, Paul. "Muddy Road," in *Zen Flesh, Zen Bones*, Page 151-152. New York City, 1957.

Enlightened-Spirituality.org. "Brother Disciples." Last modified 2006. http://www.enlightened-spirituality.org/Zen_Humor.html.

Watts, Alan. 2006. *Eastern Wisdom, Modern Life: Collected Talks: 1960-1969*. San Francisco: New World Library.

Zen Koans. "Is That So?" Accessed June, 15, 2016. http://www.ashidakim.com/zenkoans/3isthatso.html.

WORKS CONSULTED

Bhaktivedanta Swami Prabhupada, A.C. 1990. *The Bhagavad-Gita As It Is*. Los Angeles: Bhaktivedanta Book Trust.

Brunn, Joanne E. 2004. *Awakening Your Psychic Skills: Using Your Intuition to Guide Your Life*. London: Godsfield Press Ltd.

David-Neel, Alexandra and Albert Arthur Yongden. 1967. *The Secret Oral Teachings in Tibetan Buddhist Sects*. San Francisco: City Lights Books.

de Bono, Edward. 1996. *Teach Yourself to Think*. London: Penguin Books UK.

Gibran, Kahlil. 1923. *The Prophet*. New York: Alfred A. Knopf.

Greene, Robert. 2012. *Mastery*. New York: Viking Press, Penguin Books.

Haanel, Charles. 1916. *The Master Key System*. St. Louis: Psychology Publishing.

Hicks, Jerry and Esther Hicks. 2006. *The Law of Attraction: The Basics of the Teachings of Abraham.* Carlsbad: Hay House.

Holiday, Ryan. 2014. *The Obstacle is the Way: The Timeless Art of Turning Trials into Triumph.* New York: Portfolio.

Krishnamurti, Jiddu. 1975. *Freedom from the Known.* New York: HarperCollins.

LaBerge, Stephen. 2009. *Lucid Dreaming: A Concise Guide to Awakening in Your Dreams and in Your Life.* Louisville: Sounds True, Incorporated.

Lee, Bruce. 2000. *Striking Thoughts.* North Clarendon: Tuttle Publishing.

Losier, Michael J. 2003. *Law of Attraction.* New York: Grand Central Life & Style.

Orlick, Terry. 2000. *In Pursuit of Excellence: 3rd Edition.* Windsor: Human Kinetics Publishers.

Osho. 2003. *Secrets of Yoga.* Gurgaon: Penguin Books India Pvt Ltd.

Purushothaman, D. 2014. *1001 Buddhist Thoughts.* Kollam: Centre for Human Perfection.

Sanders, Michael. 2015. *Ayahuasca: An Executive's Enlightenment.* CITY: Sage & Feather Press.

Thich Nhat Hanh. 1992. *Peace Is In Every Step: The Path of Mindfulness in Everyday Life*. New York: Bantam Books, Random House.

Tolle, Eckhart. 2008. *A New Earth: Awakening to Your Life's Purpose*. New York: Penguin Books.

Tzu, Lao. 2007. *Tao Te Ching*. Toronto: Penguin Random House Canada.

Unbeatable Mind. Accessed February, 10, 2016. http://unbeatablemind.com/.

Watts, Alan. 1957. *The Way of Zen*. New York: Random House USA Inc.

Watts, Alan. 2003. *Become What You Are*. Boulder: Shambhala Publications.

Yogananda, Paramahansa. 1971. *Autobiography of a Yogi*. Los Angeles: Self-Realization Fellowship.

WOULD YOU LIKE A FREE GIFT?

Thank you so much for becoming a part of the Zen Athlete family and taking the time to learn more about the mental game of sport and life. If you liked the book, I would love to send you a secret FREE gift of your choosing. There are 3 Easy steps.

1. Take a photo of the book and post to your Facebook wall with a short caption about a favourite chapter or something you learned.

2. Go to www.amazon.com and leave a review for Zen Athlete.

3. Send a screenshot to Matt @ZenAthlete.com and let me know what sport you do and what top 3 products you would love most from www.zenathlete.com. Something to your liking will be sent. ;)

Now just Sit back, relax and continue being awesome!

www.ZenAthlete.com
www.MattBelair.com

ZEN ATHLETE

ZEN ATHLETE.com

FOLLOW US ON SOCIAL MEDIA:

Zen Athlete   @Zen_Athlete   @ZenAthlete
Matt Belair   @Matt_Belair   @MattBelair

ZEN ATHLETE.com

Explore all of the Peak Performance Training
Audio's at the official Zen Athlete website

Perfect Day Programmer   Snowboard Halfpipe Mastery

Complete Zen   Complete Zen   Complete
Skateboarding   Snowboarding   Zen Athlete
Program   Program   Program

Guided   Zen Athlete   Mental Training
Relaxation Series   Binaural Beats   Mastery Video Course

More Books From

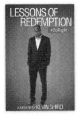

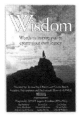

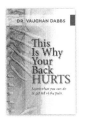

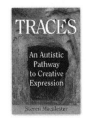

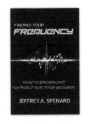

Your Book Here

www.PerfectPublishing.com